D1061643

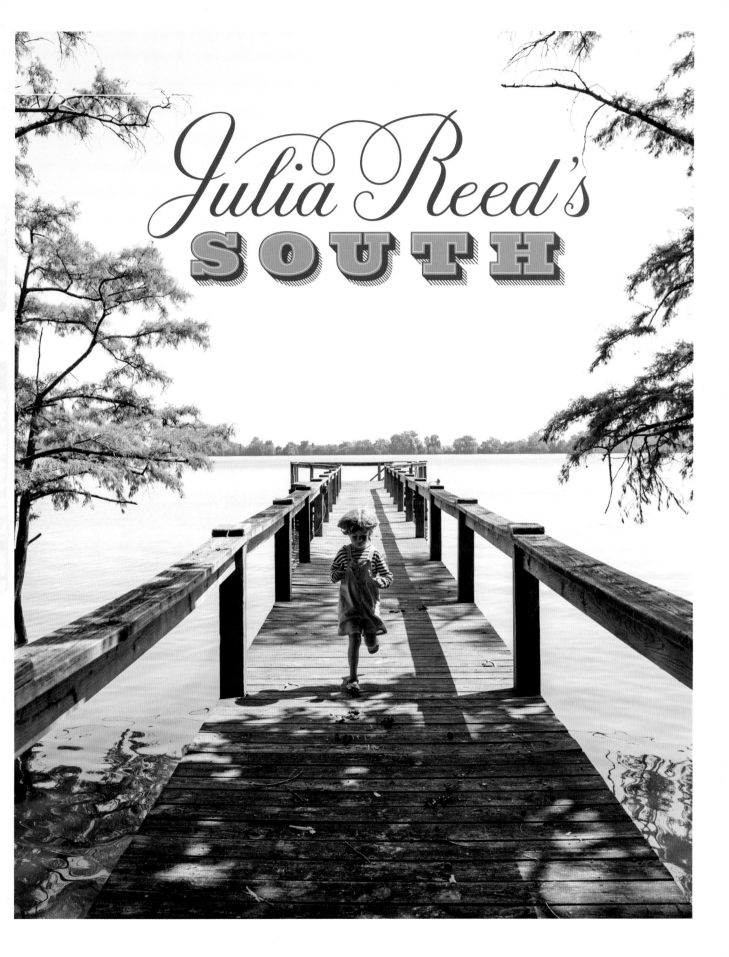

Julia Reed's SOUTH

Julia Reed's SOUTH

SPIRITED ENTERTAINING AND HIGH-STYLE FUN ALL YEAR LONG

by

JULIA REED

Photography by

PAUL COSTELLO

R*IZZOLI*
NEW YORK

New York · Paris · London · Milan

CONTENTS

Introduction   7

The Recipes

It's Finally Spring Lunch   11

Cold Creole Supper   33

Summer Celebration on the Lawn   53

Dinner on the Half Shell   75

Tomatopalooza   89

A Mississippi Sandbar Picnic   113

A Fall Hunt Breakfast   129

The Visiting Dignitary Dinner   141

A Jeffersonian Evening   161

A Christmas Cocktail Supper   177

Duck Dinner at Hollywood Plantation   197

Sources   218

Index   220

INTRODUCTION

I grew up in the Mississippi Delta, where entertaining at home was a way of life—by necessity. My hometown of Greenville is the largest city in the 6,200-plus square miles that make up the region (a diamond-shape alluvial floodplain that stretches from Memphis, Tennessee, to Vicksburg, Mississippi), which meant that there was a country club and a handful of restaurants (including the legendary steak-and-hot-tamale joint Doe's Eat Place) that we frequented. But, for the most part, if we wanted to have some fun, we learned early on how to make it ourselves. Fortunately, I had some very good teachers.

The parties of my next-door neighbors, the photojournalists Bern and Franke Keating, were so full of good-looking characters and amusing scenes that the babysitter and I watched them like movies—me from a perch in the pear tree just on the other side of the fence that divided our properties, she from a chair in front of the gap where we'd removed a plank. Our favorite guest invariably made his entrance by parachute from a Piper Cub. Such was his precision that his hosts marked his landing spot with a martini glass, and I never saw him miss.

My parents, Clarke and Judy Reed, were also (and are still) consummate entertainers and charming hosts. My childhood birthday parties were such festive affairs that when I was eleven, I decided to return the favor with a birthday dinner for my mother. I made a quiche lorraine from her copy of *Mastering the Art of French Cooking* and put surprise balls at the places of the gracious grown-up guests, who gamely unwound their crepe paper favors.

My party giving got going in earnest when I attended college in Washington, D.C., where I also worked at *Newsweek*. My endeavors were aided immensely by the game-changing publication of *The Chez Panisse Menu Cookbook*; Time Life's *The Good Cook* series, edited by the late great Richard Olney; and the food section of the now departed *House & Garden*. But the book that had the greatest impact was *Lee Bailey's Country Weekends,* featuring menus and photographs of relaxed food at the homes of Bailey's friends who, like him, had weekend places on Long Island.

Bailey grew up in Bunkie, Louisiana, but by the time I discovered him, he lived in Manhattan and had a chic housewares boutique at Henri Bendel. He went on to write seventeen more volumes about entertaining, but it was his first book that freed me to celebrate my roots. At that point, *Gourmet*'s hyper-styled vignettes were what most hostesses aspired to, and nouvelle cuisine was beginning to rear its overwrought head. In contrast, Bailey's book sported a subtitle, "Recipes for Good Food and Easy Living," that echoed the sage advice my mother had given me when I was agonizing over an especially pretentious menu: "Why don't you just serve something that tastes really good?" Bailey dazzled the jaded Hamptonites with stuff like corn bread and gumbo, grits soufflé and peach cobbler. At one of my very first D.C. dinners, I served his steamed okra with chunky tomato vinaigrette alongside Giuliano Bugialli's fancy rolled veal loin with green peppercorns and sage, and my mother's curried rice salad with marinated artichoke hearts. With

that one meal, I learned the art of mixing the high and the low on the same menu.

In this book, I hope to impart some of Bailey's spirit, as well, of course, as that of my parents and their fun-loving cohorts. In her foreword to *Country Weekends*, Amy Gross wrote that "going to Lee's is like going home, when going home is what it's cracked up to be." To me, going home still means going to the Delta, and many of the parties on these pages took place there. Others occurred in my current home, New Orleans, where I've lived off and on for twenty-five years, and in various spiritual homes, including the gardens and houses of close friends.

No matter what the location, the best reason to have a party is to have a good time, to bring together people you already love or want to know better, and, hopefully, to eat and drink well in the bargain. The only official pointer I have is pretty instinctive: taste your food. I once asked Le Bernardin's amazing Eric Ripert if he tasted as he cooked. By way of an answer, he pulled a spoon from his shirt pocket. I'm sure I swooned. So taste, and taste some more. Unlike Ripert, I'm not a chef and not nearly as exact. You might like more or less oil in your vinaigrette than I do, or a lot more pepper. When I cook, I have a heavy hand with booze, garlic, Worcestershire sauce, and, usually, salt. Speaking of the latter, when I urge a specific kind (as in kosher or flaky sea salt), I say it—the rest of the time you can use whatever you have on hand, including plain old Morton's. Likewise, when a brand (Lea & Perrin's, Pepperidge Farm) makes a difference, I include it.

The main thing is that it *all* should be a pleasure—the planning, the list-making of guests and groceries, the decoration of your table, even if you have time only for a bowl of fruit or a couple of low cylinders of grocery store roses. Celebrations, whether you're throwing a picnic on a sandbar or having a "visiting dignitary" to dinner, should not be about pomp or pretension—or even precision. A certain amount of pizzazz never hurts, and neither does generosity—not in terms of how fine the wine or expensive the caviar, but in terms of spirit. It also helps to keep a certain amount of perspective. If the host or hostess is relaxed, the guests will be too. My favorite photo in Bailey's *City Foods* is the one in which a flan has a crack down the middle.

The Delta was a wild and uninhabited place until well into the nineteenth century. Greenville has been all but wiped out twice by floods and once by the Union army. We still bear the mark of our rough-and-tumble history and remain at the mercy of the land and the river. If there's a lesson we've learned, it's that life is short. There's joy to be had. You just need to summon the *willingness* to find it. So make some cocktails, heat up the cheese dreams, and phone up your friends and neighbors.

The
Recipes

IT'S FINALLY
SPRING LUNCH

The house where I grew up in Greenville, Mississippi, is situated on six acres originally part of a cattle and farming operation called Locust Plantation and fronted by the old Rattlesnake Bayou, which once supplied water for the whole town. Though the rattlesnakes remain in all too ample evidence, the mention of those inhospitable inhabitants doubtless made early home buyers nervous, and our still country road's name was long ago shortened to simply Bayou. An 1840s slave-built levee fronts the property and serves as a tangible reminder of both the dangers of the Delta and the misdeeds of our past. Built long before the U.S. Army Corps of Engineers designed our national levee system, that original levee was the only thing protecting people, livestock, and crops from the Mississippi River—and, therefore, a pretty big deal. My mother led the fight to get the builders' efforts acknowledged with a historic marker, which, naturally, has since been stolen. But the levee itself still stands, and each spring the stretch in front of our house is covered with the tiny sweet-smelling yellow daffodils Mama brought from her own childhood home in Nashville.

Pretty much the whole front lawn beyond is also planted with thousands of bulbs in countless varieties, including the lovely all-white Thalia and the showy Fortissimo that so brilliantly complements the corn cakes with trout roe that start off our menu. The daffodils come up before most of the trees start to bud, and they've always been my favorite harbinger of the season. We may be in Mississippi, but it gets plenty cold—most years the bayou freezes over—so all those buttery blooms are a welcome sight, as well as the perfect backdrop for a first-of-spring lunch.

Spring's edible harbingers include, first and foremost, asparagus, a discovery I happily made when our next-door neighbor, the late writer Bern Keating, added an asparagus bed to his already-extensive vegetable garden. I was nine, I think, and until then, I'd known only of the not entirely unpleasant, saline-infused sticks

Daffodils have always been my favorite harbinger of the season.

of gray-green mush available year-round from Del Monte or Green Giant. My first-picked young spear from Bern's bed was a revelation. Lamb, too, is a spring thing, and our menu's simple roast, flavored—but not overly so—with herbs and a little garlic is a permanent fixture on my Easter table. Crabs also begin their peak season when the weather gets warm, so I include a crab soup, enlivened with more tender herbs, as a first course, and for dessert, there's a sort of deconstructed and amplified ambrosia. My father grew up eating that unembellished mixture of citrus and coconut, and it was one of the two desserts in my paternal grandmother's tiny arsenal. But as a kid, I could never get the point of it. I much preferred her other inevitable Easter offering—a moist coconut cake in the shape of a bunny, complete with pink paper ears and a licorice jelly bean nose. I miss Kay (whom I only ever called by her first name, short for Kathryn—she was as straightforward as the ambrosia she made), and every year I miss that sweet cake. This dessert is my tribute to her.

The Menu

Champagne Cocktails
with Grapefruit Bitters

Corn Cakes
with Crème Fraîche and Trout Roe

Creole Crab Soup

Roast Boneless Leg of Lamb
with Herbs

Mock Cheese Soufflé

Asparagus
with Brown Butter Vinaigrette

Almond Polenta Cake
*with Coconut Ice Cream
and Candied Citrus*

A NOTE ON THE
TABLE SETTING & THE WINES

Almost every female in my mother's family is named either Frances or Julia. My first cousin Brooks, whose sister and mother were both named Frances, even married a Frances (a fact we don't think needs clinical examination, because she happens to be wonderful). Anyway, it's a state of affairs that makes things really easy when dividing up the monogrammed linens. During the last divvying-up session, I got a mint green–and-white damask tablecloth and matching napkins that all but cry out for use in spring. The green parts of the damask are woven to reveal a pair of deer at play, and the monogram is that of my beloved maternal grandmother, Julia Clements Brooks.

For china, I paired Herend's Rothschild Bird pattern (first created in 1860 for the Rothschild family) with pieces from an antique yellow, gold, and white set. I got the latter just before I canceled what would have been my first wedding (the set was a gift from my grandfather, who graciously allowed me to keep it anyway), and the former I got years later when I finally did marry. I am a sucker for anything involving birds or a good story, and the Herend has both. After Baroness Rothschild lost a pearl necklace in the garden of her Vienna residence, a gardener spotted birds playing with it in a tree, and the tale is depicted in twelve different vignettes on the plates. They, too, are perfect for spring, as are the wines chosen with excellent advice from my friend Byron Seward.

Byron is a widely respected farmer who grows cotton, corn, and soybeans near Yazoo City, Mississippi, the kind of place where you need your own wine cellar, especially if you're blessed with Byron's palate. For the first course, he came up with a Spanish Albariño, specifically a Palacio de Fefiñanes Albariño III Años 2011 or 2014. It's got just enough salinity and acidity for a rich shellfish like crab—especially crab in a lemony, tomatoey broth. You could also go with a more typical white Burgundy—my Chardonnay-loving mother prefers a Meursault with this soup, and I am always happy to comply. For the lamb, Byron chose a 2006 La Migoua, one of the three reds produced by Provence's famed Domaine Tempier, a great favorite of us both. But because it's spring, he also suggested a white wine I adore, Château Beaucastel Châteauneuf-du-Pape Blanc Roussanne Vieilles Vignes 2013. Rich and lush and full of fruit, it also has a lively minerality and even a touch of Meyer lemon that make it nothing short of mind-blowing with the lamb. It's definitely worth a search.

Champagne Cocktails
with Grapefruit Bitters

could could never get on board with a classic Champagne cocktail because I find the called-for Angostura bitters far too strident with the wine. Then, a few years ago, I discovered this lovely light (and totally addictive) version made with grapefruit bitters at Bar Tonique, one of my favorite New Orleans watering holes. Now I'm a proselytizer.

Put a sugar cube at the bottom of each of six Champagne flutes and douse each cube with a few drops of bitters. Fill the flutes with Champagne and garnish each with a strip of grapefruit zest. You can get fancy and make elaborate corkscrews, but I just take a vegetable peeler and shave off 1-inch pieces of the zest.

Serves 6

6 sugar cubes, such as La Perruche brand

Fee Brothers Grapefruit Bitters (see Sources, page 219)

1 bottle Champagne

Six 1-inch pieces of zest from 1 ripe grapefruit for garnish

Corn Cakes
with Crème Fraîche & Trout Roe

If I could eat only one thing for the rest of my life, it would be blini with ossetra caviar, but these far-more-affordable canapés are a close second. They're also better suited to our menu. To me, roe equals rebirth equals spring, and the color is extraordinary. I love the mouthfeel of the firmer trout eggs, but salmon roe works just as well. And if you can't get your hands on crème fraîche, don't fret—sour cream is a fine alternative, especially if you add a few drops of lemon juice.

If using frozen corn kernels, thaw and drain them before adding them to the bowl of a food processor. If using fresh, scrape them directly into the bowl of a food processor along with their milk. Pulse just until you have a rough puree—you want to retain some of the kernels' texture.

Combine the cornmeal, flour, salt, sugar, baking powder, and white pepper in a medium bowl. In another medium bowl, whisk together the egg, egg yolk, cream, and cooled melted butter. Add the egg mixture to the cornmeal mixture and stir until smooth. Fold in the corn puree.

In a large skillet, melt the remaining 1 tablespoon butter and the vegetable oil over medium-high heat. Add 1 heaping tablespoon batter per corn cake to the pan and cook until the cakes are golden, 1 to 2 minutes on each side. Add more butter and/or oil if needed.

Arrange the corn cakes on a platter. Spread each with 1 to 2 teaspoons of the crème fraîche and top with a dollop of the roe.

Makes about 24 canapés

2 cups frozen or fresh corn kernels

½ cup yellow cornmeal

½ cup all-purpose flour

1 teaspoon salt

1 teaspoon sugar

½ teaspoon baking powder

⅛ teaspoon freshly ground white pepper

1 large egg, beaten

1 large egg yolk

¾ cup heavy cream

3 tablespoons butter, melted and cooled, plus 1 tablespoon for cooking

1 tablespoon vegetable oil

1 cup crème fraîche

One 250-gram tin trout or salmon roe

Creole Crab Soup

I n this chapter, I'm a bit of a stock nudge. Though I've made this soup many times with store-bought seafood stock, a reduced homemade shrimp stock really "kicks it up a notch," to borrow Emeril's favorite phrase, and it's so easy it's ridiculous. Not only will you have a yummier soup, you'll have two pounds of shelled shrimp to play with for lunch or dinner.

Using a vegetable peeler, remove the zest from 1 lemon in one long strip, if possible. Juice the peeled lemon and set the juice aside. Thinly slice the remaining lemon crosswise into 6 slices and set aside.

Melt the butter in a large deep skillet or Dutch oven over medium heat. Add the onion and garlic and sauté until soft, about 4 minutes. Add the tomatoes and the stock and turn the heat up to medium-high. When the mixture boils, turn the heat down to maintain a simmer. Add the bay leaf, parsley, marjoram, 2 tablespoons of the mint, the tarragon, lemon zest strip, and 1½ tablespoons of the lemon juice. Simmer, partly covered, for 30 to 45 minutes.

Add the crabmeat and simmer gently until the soup is slightly thickened, about 10 minutes. Add salt and cayenne to taste, and more lemon juice, if needed. Discard the bay leaf, parsley, and marjoram. Add the remaining 1 tablespoon mint at the last minute. After you spoon the soup into bowls, top each serving with a lemon slice.

NOTE: *If you use store-bought stock, reserve the juice from the canned tomatoes and add it to the stock.*

Serves 6 as an appetizer

2 large lemons

3 tablespoons butter

1 medium yellow onion, finely chopped

2 minced garlic cloves

3 cups canned whole peeled tomatoes, seeded and chopped

4 cups store-bought seafood stock or Homemade Shrimp Stock (page 22)

1 bay leaf

2 Italian parsley sprigs

1 marjoram sprig

3 tablespoons finely chopped mint leaves

1 tablespoon finely chopped tarragon leaves

1 pound jumbo lump crabmeat

Salt

Cayenne pepper

Homemade Shrimp Stock

Makes 5 to 6 cups

2 pounds shrimp,
    preferably with the
    heads still attached
1 tablespoon olive oil
8 cups water
Generous pinch of salt

Remove the shrimp shells and heads, reserving the shrimp for another use. In a large pot, heat the olive oil over medium heat. Add the shrimp shells and heads and sauté—both stirring and shaking the pot to make sure the shells don't scorch—for 3 to 4 minutes, until the shells turn a deep pink. Add the water and salt and bring the mixture to a boil over high heat. Turn down the heat and simmer, partially covered, for 1 hour.

Strain the stock into a smaller pot and cook to reduce the liquid by at least 1 cup, until it's a pretty red color and tastes like intensified ocean!

Homemade Lamb Stock

Makes about 6 cups

1 pound lamb bones
4 tablespoons olive oil
1 large yellow onion,
    roughly chopped
1 carrot, diced
1 celery stalk, diced
4 garlic cloves, smashed
1 tablespoon tomato paste
½ cup dry white wine
4 to 6 cups water
4 or 5 thyme sprigs
4 or 5 Italian parsley sprigs
2 bay leaves
2 teaspoons whole black
    peppercorns

Preheat the oven to 425°F. Place the lamb bones in a roasting pan, drizzle with 2 tablespoons of the olive oil, and roast for 1 hour, turning the bones halfway through the cooking.

Meanwhile, in a deep stockpot, heat the remaining 2 tablespoons oil over medium-high heat. Add the onion, carrot, and celery and sauté, stirring occasionally, until they're browned, about 8 minutes. Stir in the garlic and tomato paste and cook for another 3 minutes. Add the white wine, making sure to scrape the bottom of the pot with a spoon, and let boil until the liquid has reduced by half.

Add the roasted bones and water and bring the mixture to a boil, skimming off any foam that rises to the top. Add the thyme, parsley, bay leaves, and peppercorns and simmer for at least 4 hours.

Let the stock cool off for a bit, strain through a fine-mesh sieve, and refrigerate overnight. Lift off the hardened fat and, when ready to use, bring to a simmer.

NOTE: *I often double or even triple the recipes and freeze these stocks in individual 1- or 2-cup containers. Use frozen stock within 3 months.*

Roasted Boneless Leg of Lamb
with Herbs

Serves 8 to 10

One 4-pound leg of lamb, boned, butterflied, and trimmed of all but a thin layer of fat

2 tablespoons olive oil

1 tablespoon fresh lemon juice

2 garlic cloves, crushed and finely chopped

3 teaspoons finely chopped rosemary leaves

1 tablespoon minced thyme leaves

1 tablepoon chopped marjoram leaves

Kosher salt and freshly ground black pepper

1 cup Homemade Lamb Stock (page 22) or store-bought chicken stock

½ cup dry white wine or vermouth

This roast doesn't require a sauce, but one made from the pan juices really elevates the dish. And the sauce itself is really elevated by using homemade lamb stock. Just get the butcher to give you the bones from the lamb, and you could also add a shank or two from his case.

One day before roasting the lamb, spread it out as flat as possible and rub the exposed side all over with 1 tablespoon of the olive oil, the lemon juice, garlic, rosemary, thyme, marjoram, and salt and pepper to taste. Roll the meat into a cylinder like a jelly roll and secure with pieces of butcher string, tying a knot every 1½ inches from end to end. Rub the exterior with the remaining 1 tablespoon oil and more salt and pepper. Cover and refrigerate.

Remove the lamb from the refrigerator at least 3 hours before cooking. Preheat the oven to 325°F.

Place the lamb in a shallow roasting pan not much larger than the meat. Place the pan in the center of the oven and roast undisturbed for 1 hour. Use a thermometer to check the meat's temperature: It should be at least 100°F. For medium-rare meat, roast until the temperature is 125°F, 10 to 15 minutes more.

Remove the lamb from the roasting pan and let rest for 15 minutes before slicing. Meanwhile, skim off as much fat as possible from the pan and set the pan over two burners on low heat. Add the stock and white wine, scraping the pan to loosen the brown bits, and increase the heat to high. Reduce the sauce, stirring, for 8 to 10 minutes. Drizzle over sliced lamb or pass in a sauceboat at the table.

Mock Cheese Soufflé

This "soufflé"—in reality a bread pudding—is so super easy to prepare it's crazy. People are always dazzled because not only does it have the consistency of a soufflé, it still looks beautiful by the time it gets to the table. The trick is to buy the best Cheddar you can find. I've made it with Cracker Barrel, but it's really sublime with Cabot Clothbound.

Preheat the oven to 350°F. Butter an 8-cup soufflé dish.

Butter each slice of bread on one side and cut into 4 squares. Layer half the bread, buttered side up, in the bottom of the dish. Cover with half the grated Cheddar and repeat.

Combine the eggs, salt, milk, Worcestershire sauce, and cayenne in a large bowl and mix well. Pour the egg mixture over the bread and cheese. (At this point, the "soufflé" can be refrigerated for up to 1 day.)

Bake on the center rack until the top is browned and the soufflé is bubbling around the edges, about 45 minutes. Serve immediately.

Serves 6 as a side dish, 4 as a main dish

Softened butter for greasing the dish and spreading on bread

8 slices firm white bread, such as Pepperidge Farm, crusts removed

1 pound sharp Cheddar cheese, grated

4 large eggs, beaten

½ teaspoon salt

2 cups whole milk

2 teaspoons Lea & Perrins Worcestershire sauce

Pinch of cayenne pepper

Asparagus
with Brown Butter Vinaigrette

Serves 6 to 8

3 to 4 pounds asparagus

6 ounces (1½ sticks) butter

6 tablespoons olive oil

2 tablespoons finely chopped shallots

2 tablespoons drained capers

1 tablespoon finely chopped cornichons

1 tablespoon finely chopped Italian parsley leaves

3 tablespoons sherry vinegar

3 tablespoons fresh lemon juice

Kosher salt and freshly ground black pepper

I put this vinaigrette on lots of stuff, from grilled or poached fish to sliced boiled fingerling potatoes for a terrific potato salad. But I especially like its nutty taste with the herby asparagus.

Snap off the tough ends of the asparagus (you will be able to feel where it should break).

Melt the butter in a small saucepan or skillet over medium heat. When it starts to foam, stir to keep the milk solids from sticking to the bottom of the pan. (Watch it carefully! I've had to start over more than once.) In 4 to 5 minutes, the butter should be brown (not burned) and give off a nutty aroma. Remove from the heat and set aside.

In another skillet, heat the olive oil over medium heat. Add the shallots and sauté for 2 to 3 minutes, until they begin to soften. Turn up the heat to medium-high, add the capers, and shake the pan or stir for a couple of minutes until the capers are a bit crunchy. Stir in the cornichons and parsley and remove from the heat.

Combine the butter and the olive oil mixture in a small bowl. Whisk in the vinegar and lemon juice, and add salt and pepper to taste.

Bring a large pot of water to a boil, over high heat. Add a generous pinch of salt and the asparagus. Return to a boil, and cook until the asparagus is tender, 3 to 5 minutes. Drain the asparagus and spread the spears out on a cookie sheet lined with paper towels or a dish towel.

To serve, place the asparagus on a platter or individual plates and spoon the vinaigrette over.

Almond Polenta Cake
with Coconut Ice Cream and Candied Citrus

I used to make homemade coconut ice cream to serve with this until I discovered Talenti Caribbean Coconut gelato and realized I was wasting my time. That stuff is delicious and widely available. If you can't find it, feel free to get out your ice cream maker, but you could also garnish with whipped cream and some toasted coconut instead.

TO MAKE THE CAKE

Preheat the oven to 325°F. Butter and flour two 9-inch cake pans and set aside.

In the bowl of a stand mixer fitted with the whisk attachment, beat the butter and sugar on high speed until pale and light, 1 to 2 minutes. Add the almond meal and vanilla and mix well. Beat in the eggs, one at a time. Using a large spoon, stir in the lemon zest, lemon juice, orange zest, orange juice, corn flour, cornmeal, baking powder, and salt until just combined.

Pour the batter into the prepared pans and bake until the cakes are set and a deep golden brown on top, about 40 minutes. Cool on a wire rack.

TO MAKE THE CANDIED CITRUS

Peel the citrus and separate the fruit into segments, removing as much pith as possible. Set aside.

Bring the sugar and water to a boil in a medium saucepan over high heat, stirring to make sure the sugar dissolves. Reduce the heat to low, add the citrus segments, and simmer for about 5 minutes, until they've puffed up a bit.

Strain the mixture through a fine-mesh sieve into a medium bowl and return the liquid to the saucepan. Set the pan over medium-high heat and cook until the syrup is thick enough to coat the back of a spoon, 6 to 8 minutes. Allow to cool completely, then gently stir in the citrus segments. (These may be stored, covered, in the refrigerator for up to 3 days.)

To serve, cut the cake into wedges and accompany each piece with a scoop of gelato, about ¼ cup of the candied citrus, and a sprig of mint.

Serves 12

FOR THE CAKE

1 pound (4 sticks) butter, plus more for greasing the pans

All-purpose flour for dusting the pans

2 cups plus 1 tablespoon sugar

4 cups almond meal or finely ground blanched almonds

2 teaspoons pure vanilla extract

6 large eggs

Grated zest of **4** lemons, plus juice of **1** lemon

Grated zest of **1** orange, plus juice of **1** orange

½ cup corn flour

½ cup cornmeal

1½ teaspoons baking powder

¼ teaspoon salt

FOR THE CANDIED CITRUS

8 clementines, mandarin oranges, tangerines, or tangelos

1½ cups sugar

1 cup water

Mint sprigs for garnish

COLD CREOLE SUPPER

During the seventeenth- and eighteenth-century rule by the French and the Spanish in Louisiana, the term "Creole" was used to distinguish between those "born away" and those born on native soil. Because the latter encompassed both African Americans and Native Americans as well as Europeans, the moniker transcended ethnicity and race and came to apply not only to the people but also to the happy results of the mixing and mingling of their food—notably Creole cuisine. These days there are almost as many definitions of Creole as there are those who go by the description, but the broad delineation still applies: A Creole is anyone whose ancestors were born in colonial Louisiana.

An even broader definition is "product of the provinces," which can include everything from a Creole tomato, grown (supposedly) with seeds from the colonial period, to my friend Peter Patout, a New Orleans–based antiques dealer and realtor specializing in historic houses, whose family came here three centuries ago to plant sugarcane. At this point, Peter says, he's got some Acadian blood and who knows what else: "We've been over here three hundred years; we're gonna have it all." It's a line that can also apply to Creole cooking, which has been enlivened over the years by contributions from the area's ever-expanding culture. Italian immigrants brought red gravy, and Paul Prudhomme famously infused Creole with Cajun, but the constants are the use of ingredients found in southern Louisiana and a nod, however brief, to French haute cuisine.

I met Peter in his former shop more than two decades ago, and he's been my fast friend and stalwart guide ever since. We've been to countless honky-tonks hidden in the cane fields; we've watched sugar being processed in the Patoutville mill, near New Iberia. Out there, we mostly eat Cajun gumbos made with a dark roux; in New Orleans, he feeds me his aunt Evelyn's crab stew, made Creole style with tomatoes and no roux.

Peter owns a magical compound at the bottom end of Bourbon Street made up of an early Creole cottage and a Victorian double shotgun house separated by a small courtyard. There's not a kitchen bigger than a closet anywhere on the premises, but somehow Peter manages to entertain fearlessly, and I could think of no more perfect spot to host a Creole supper.

The Menu

Pimm's Royale

**Grilled Deviled Crab &
Cheese Sandwiches**

Fried Oysters
in Romaine Canoes

Daube Glacé

Shrimp Rémoulade

Celery Root Rémoulade

Haricots Verts
with Shallot Vinaigrette

**Café au Lait
Pots de Créme**

A NOTE ON THE TABLE SETTING

Peter is a master of scale and has always made gutsy pieces work in his relatively small spaces. In his narrow shotgun house, there's no space for a proper dining room, but he manages to squeeze in a table big enough to accommodate six or eight by using the handsome Regency banquette against the wall as seating on one side. The table is covered in a toile that depicts the Louisiana Purchase and was made by our friend Roulhac Toledano and her company Architextiles (see Sources, page 219). The plates are gold-and-white "Old Paris," a loose term that applies to gilded and painted porcelain tableware and other accessories created in and around Paris from the mid-1700s through the end of the Second Empire. The French stemmed glassware was hand blown in the early nineteenth century.

A NOTE ON THE WINE

During dinner, depending on the taste of the drinkers, the glasses contained a Domaine Lucien Crochet Sancerre or a light red Burgundy from the Côte de Nuit. With dessert we served—what else?—the New Orleans Special Reserve Madeira from The Rare Wine Co.'s Historic Series. Each wine in the series is named for a city where Madeira was popular in the eighteenth and nineteenth centuries, and this one is rich and nutty, with flavors of oranges and brown sugar that pair perfectly with the silky, coffee-flavored crèmes.

Pimm's Royale

Serves 1

1¾ ounces Pimm's No. 1
Brut Champagne
1 cucumber spear, unpeeled
1 lime slice
1 orange slice
1 mint sprig for garnish
1 or 2 brandied cherries for garnish

A Sazerac, invented in New Orleans and said to be the first cocktail, would seem the obvious choice to kick off a Creole supper, but the Pimm's Cup is also strongly identified with the city. For as long as anyone can remember, this quintessentially British cooler has been the signature drink at the fabled Napoleon House. A cocktail served at Wimbledon is an odd choice for an establishment named for an emperor whose literal undoing came at the hands of a British general. But no one questions it, and now countless Pimm's variations, including one with watermelon syrup, are available in bars across town. I discovered my own favorite variation, the Pimm's Royale, years ago at the Paris Ritz, another decidedly un-English outpost. Crisp, refreshing, and seriously delicious, it has ranked among my favorite cocktails ever since. Even better, the use of Champagne as its mixer eliminates all the pesky sparring over whether ginger ale, sparkling lemonade, or 7UP is the proper choice. The only decision here is the cherry. The Ritz uses brandied cherries, which I prefer, but Luxardo gourmet maraschinos are a good second option.

Fill a goblet or highball glass with ice. Add the Pimm's, top with Champagne, and add the cucumber spear, lime slice, orange slice, mint sprig, and cherries.

Grilled Deviled Crab
& Cheese Sandwiches

Makes about 15 sandwich triangles

4 tablespoons (½ stick) butter, plus more for grilling

1 cup finely diced andouille sausage

1 medium yellow onion, finely chopped (about 1 cup)

¼ cup thinly sliced scallions, including some of the green tops

¾ cup heavy cream

¼ cup grated Parmesan cheese

¾ cup grated good Cheddar cheese

1 teaspoon Tabasco sauce

1½ teaspoons Lea & Perrins Worcestershire sauce

1 large egg yolk

1 pound lump crabmeat, picked over for shells and patted dry

2 teaspoons fresh lemon juice

1 loaf Pepperidge Farm Very Thin Sliced White Bread

½ cup finely minced Italian parsley or chives, or a mixture of both

Both these sandwiches and the fried oysters that follow on page 43 belie the title of this menu, but when the main meal is entirely cold, I like to give people something hot and crunchy or hot and cheesy beforehand. I first tasted a version of this luscious, highly seasoned crabmeat, which certainly fulfills the latter criteria, as a filling for pastry turnovers. But the buttery, toasty bread provides a far more simpatico delivery system and makes the ultimate grilled cheese sandwich.

Melt the butter in a skillet over medium heat. Add the sausage and fry for 5 minutes. Drain off all but 1 tablespoon of the fat. Add the onion and sauté until soft, about 8 minutes. Add the scallions, cream, Parmesan, Cheddar, Tabasco, and Worcestershire sauce and stir until the mixture is bubbling and thickened, about 8 minutes. Remove from the heat.

Beat the egg yolk in a large bowl. Gradually add about 1 cup of the cheese mixture, mix well, and stir in the rest. Toss the crab in the lemon juice and fold it into the filling. Taste for seasoning and refrigerate, covered with plastic wrap, for at least 1 hour before making the sandwiches. (At this point the filling may be refrigerated overnight.)

To make the sandwiches: Cut the crusts off the bread, spread a layer of crab filling between 2 slices, press them together, and repeat. In a large skillet, melt 1 tablespoon butter over medium heat. Place as many of the sandwiches in the skillet as it will hold. Press down lightly with a spatula and turn over after about 2 minutes, or as soon as the underside is golden brown. Press down again and remove the sandwiches to a warm baking sheet when the flipsides have browned. As you cook, you will likely need to add more butter. If the butter gets too brown after a few batches, you may need to wipe out the pan and start over.

When all the sandwiches are done, spread the minced parsley on a plate. Cut each sandwich in half into triangles and dip the long edges into the herbs. Serve immediately.

Fried Oysters
in Romaine Canoes

My friendship with Jason Epstein, the legendary publisher and editor, has been one of the great gifts of my life—along with his tutelage in the kitchen. He introduced me to these supremely simple oysters for a casual dinner we cooked together almost fifteen years ago, and I've made them so often since then that my friends have come to expect them at almost every party. They've got that crispy/salty, hot/cold thing going on that makes a BLT so irresistible, and no matter how many times I serve them, guests still chase after the trays. This is one of those recipes people invariably try to tart up by adding actual crumbled bacon or substituting tartar sauce or homemade mayo for the Hellmann's. Don't do it. I love bacon and I'm a snob about homemade mayo, but this is the one time neither is needed nor as good.

Mix the mayonnaise, lemon juice, chives, and cayenne in a small bowl until smooth.

Cut off the bottoms of the romaine hearts and remove the outer leaves of each head. Cut into fourteen to sixteen 1-inch "canoes." Arrange the canoes on a serving platter and top each with a dollop of the mayonnaise mixture. Set aside while frying the oysters.

Drain the oysters. Spread the cornmeal on a cookie sheet. Dredge the oysters in the cornmeal, one at a time, and place in a colander, shaking off any excess cornmeal.

Heat the vegetable oil in a deep skillet over medium-high heat until it reaches 350°F. (You can also check by sprinkling some of the cornmeal in the oil. If it spins and dances, the oil should be ready.) Gently drop an oyster into the hot oil. If it doesn't rise to the top, wait a minute or two and try again. If it does, add 3 or 4 more oysters, being careful not to crowd the pan. When the oysters are a light brown, remove them with a slotted spoon to paper towels to drain, and sprinkle with the salt and white pepper to taste.

As soon as all the oysters are done, plop one on top of the mayonnaise on each of the romaine canoes. Serve immediately.

Makes 14 to 16 hors d'oeuvres

1 cup Hellmann's mayonnaise

1 tablespoon fresh lemon juice

2 tablespoons minced chives

Pinch of cayenne pepper

4 hearts of romaine

1 pint fresh-shucked oysters

1½ cups white cornmeal or unseasoned Zatarain's Fish Fri

4 cups vegetable oil

1 teaspoon salt

Freshly ground white pepper

Daube Glacé

*Serves 10 to 12
as a main course*

One 4-pound boneless beef
chuck roast

About **3** tablespoons salt

Freshly ground black pepper

¼ cup bacon grease or
vegetable oil

3 medium white onions,
thinly sliced

3 carrots, thinly sliced

1 cup diced celery

8 garlic cloves, crushed and
roughly chopped

8 Italian parsley sprigs

5 bay leaves

5 cups beef stock

½ cup dry red wine

½ cup brandy

12 whole cloves, crushed

2 teaspoons white
peppercorns

1 teaspoon dried thyme

1 teaspoon whole allspice

½ teaspoon cayenne pepper

3 tablespoons Lea & Perrins
Worcestershire sauce

1 teaspoon Tabasco sauce

1 cup water

4 tablespoons (4 envelopes
Knox) unflavored gelatin

5 tablespoons fresh lemon
juice

Daube glacé, a jellied mixture of beef and broth, was a mainstay on proper Creole tables in the eighteenth and nineteenth centuries, when boiling the feet of calves or pigs caused the dish to set. Now, of course, there's Knox, but the first time I made it—for a picnic in the British countryside—I tried the traditional route with disastrous results. The guests on that occasion included my friend the New Orleans–born interior designer Suzanne Rheinstein, who often serves daube as a canapé on sliced French bread with homemade mayonnaise. (You can also make a yummy po' boy from the same ingredients.) Here, we simply passed the extra rémoulades from the shrimp and celeriac (pages 46 and 48) as accompaniments.

Sprinkle the roast generously with about 1 tablespoon of the salt and pepper. Heat the bacon grease in a large heavy-bottomed casserole over medium-high heat. Add the roast and brown on all sides. Add the onions, carrots, celery, garlic, parsley, and bay leaves to the pan. Sauté until the vegetables are slightly softened, about 5 minutes.

Add the beef stock, red wine, brandy, cloves, peppercorns, thyme, allspice, cayenne, Worcestershire sauce, and Tabasco. Cover and bring to a simmer over medium-low heat. Reduce the heat to very low and simmer until the roast is very tender, about 3 hours, turning the meat occasionally if it's not submerged.

Remove the meat to a cutting board, reserving the cooking liquid. Let cool and cut into ½-inch slices. Break or chop into small, roughly ½-inch pieces, shredding slightly. Oil two 1½-quart loaf pans and spread half the meat over the bottom of each pan.

Pour the cooking liquid through a cheesecloth-lined strainer set over a large saucepan. Place the pan over high heat and bring to a boil. Reduce the heat slightly and cook until 1 cup of the cooking liquid has boiled away.

Place the water in a small saucepan and sprinkle with the gelatin. Set aside for 5 minutes to soften, then heat over low heat until dissolved. Stir into the reduced stock. Add 2 tablespoons salt and the lemon juice. Stir well and pour over the meat. Refrigerate until the stock is set.

To serve, remove the fat from the top of the jellied stock and unmold each loaf onto a serving platter. Slice with the sharpest knife you've got, dipped into hot water.

Shrimp Rémoulade

FOR THE CREOLE RÉMOULADE SAUCE

2 large egg yolks

¼ cup vegetable oil

¼ cup prepared horseradish

2 tablespoons Creole or any grainy French mustard

1 tablespoon Dijon mustard

½ cup finely chopped celery

½ cup finely chopped scallions

¼ cup chopped Italian parsley

¼ large lemon, seeded and cut into 3 pieces, including the rind

2 tablespoons Heinz ketchup

2 tablespoons Lea & Perrins Worcestershire sauce

1 tablespoon white wine vinegar

1 tablespoon Tabasco sauce

1 tablespoon minced garlic

2 teaspoons sweet paprika

3 tablespoons drained capers

1 teaspoon salt

1 bay leaf, crumbled

A Creole rémoulade is an entirely different—and far more loaded—concoction than a classic French "white" rémoulade, which is really nothing more than a mayonnaise with pickles, capers, anchovies, and herbs. Here, I toss the shrimp in the more robust Creole rémoulade and serve it on the same platter with grated celery root dressed in the French version. I love the juxtaposition of Old World against New, and the two sauces really complement each other. You could also try crawfish tails in the Creole sauce alongside shrimp in the French.

TO MAKE THE CREOLE RÉMOULADE SAUCE

In a blender or the bowl of a food processor, process the yolks for 2 minutes. With the machine running, add the vegetable oil in a thin stream. Then, one at a time, blend in the horseradish, Creole mustard, Dijon mustard, celery, scallions, parsley, lemon, ketchup, Worcestershire sauce, vinegar, Tabasco, garlic, paprika, capers, salt, and bay leaf until well mixed and the lemon rind is finely chopped. Transfer the sauce to a container, cover with plastic wrap, and keep refrigerated until needed. The sauce can be refrigerated for up to 1 week.

TO MAKE THE SHRIMP

Combine the water, crab boil, salt, and lemons in a large stockpot or Dutch oven and bring to a boil over high heat. Reduce the heat and simmer for 5 minutes. Turn the heat to high and add the shrimp. Cook, uncovered, for 3 minutes. Immediately drain the shrimp in the colander, discarding the seasoning bag and lemon pieces.

When the shrimp are cool enough to handle, peel them and place them in a large bowl.

TO ASSEMBLE THE DISH

Toss the shrimp with 1½ cups of the Creole rémoulade sauce. Add more as needed.

NOTE: *I'm terrified of overcooking shrimp, and I like mine just this side of cooked, so after 2 or 3 minutes, I usually grab a shrimp with tongs, run it under cold water, and take a bite in order to check the progress. Also, as soon as you dump them in the colander, toss a couple of times to keep those on the bottom from "cooking" longer.*

Celery Root Rémoulade

2 pounds celery root
(celeriac)
Juice of 2 lemons
White Rémoulade Sauce

**FOR THE WHITE
RÉMOULADE SAUCE**

1 large egg
1 tablespoon Dijon
mustard
1 teaspoon drained capers
1 teaspoon chopped
cornichons
1 anchovy, rinsed and
chopped
1 tablespoon chopped
chervil
1 tablespoon chopped
chives
1 tablespoon chopped
Italian parsley
1 tablespoon chopped
tarragon
Juice of 1 lemon, strained
1 tablespoon champagne
vinegar
1 cup vegetable oil
¼ cup olive oil
Salt

Salt and freshly ground
white pepper

Peel the celery root and cut out any deep brown grooves. Cut into large chunks and grate coarsely using a hand grater or a food processor. Place the celery root in a bowl of cold water and add the lemon juice. Let sit for 10 minutes. Drain, place in a dish towel, and squeeze out the excess moisture.

TO MAKE THE WHITE RÉMOULADE SAUCE

Place the egg, mustard, capers, cornichons, anchovy, chervil, chives, parsley, tarragon, lemon, and vinegar in a food processor. Process until very frothy. Add the vegetable oil and olive oil in a thin stream until the mixture is uniform and well blended. Taste and add salt as needed.

TO ASSEMBLE THE DISH

Place the celery root in a large bowl and mix in 1 cup of the white rémoulade sauce, adding more if it's too dry. Add salt and white pepper to taste.

Haricots Verts
with Shallot Vinaigrette

This menu cries out for something fresh and green, and these skinny green beans are the perfect thing—as well as another nod to the "mother country." When making the dressing, I like to slightly pickle the shallots first by marinating them in the vinegar for a bit, a technique I learned from the gifted chef David Tanis.

Bring a large pot of salted water to a boil over high heat. Add the beans and cook for about 4 minutes, until bright green and tender but still firm. Drain in a colander and spread out on dish towels to both dry and cool them.

Place the shallots in a small bowl and sprinkle with the vinegar and salt to taste. Let sit for about 10 minutes. Whisk in the olive oil and the 1 teaspoon salt.

Place the beans in a large bowl. Add the shallot dressing, parsley, and pepper to taste and toss well. Taste for seasonings.

Serves 8

1 teaspoon kosher salt, plus more for cooking

2 pounds small green beans (haricots verts)

3 large shallots, finely diced

3 tablespoons sherry vinegar

¾ cup olive oil

1 tablespoon chopped Italian parsley or chervil

Freshly ground black pepper

Café au Lait Pots de Crème

3 cups heavy cream

¾ cup sugar

6 tablespoons instant espresso powder

1 tablespoon brandy

1½ teaspoons pure vanilla extract

8 large egg yolks

Whipped cream for garnish

I n *Mastering the Art of French Cooking,* Julia Child and her coauthors chastise those who erroneously refer to cold mousses served in porcelain custard cups as pots de crème. Crèmes are always baked custards, and pots de crème refer to the name of the cups they're baked and served in, as well as to the dessert itself, which dates back to the seventeenth century. This version is a nod to New Orleans's beloved café brûlot, an after-dinner concoction of coffee, brandy, orange liqueur, and spices mixed tableside at such Creole temples as Arnaud's and Galatoire's. When making brûlot, the server ladles the spiked coffee down a spiral of orange peel in a maneuver that's both exciting and a tiny bit risky—a now retired waiter at Galatoire's once set our table on fire. Here, the crèmes are garnished with crumbled pralines (another local specialty) because I had them on hand, but for an even truer homage to brûlot, you could use candied orange peel instead. As for the pots themselves, my lovely Old Paris set was given to me a couple of years ago by my cherished friend and über collector Furlow Gatewood, but until that happy day, I made do with ceramic ramekins, which work just fine.

Preheat the oven to 325°F.

Heat the cream in a heavy-bottomed saucepan over medium heat until small bubbles form around the edges of the pan. Add the sugar, espresso powder, brandy, and vanilla and stir continously until the sugar and coffee have dissolved. Remove from the heat.

Place the egg yolks in a bowl and whisk until blended. Slowly add the hot cream mixture while whisking continuously to prevent curdling. Strain the mixture through a fine-mesh sieve into a pitcher and pour into eight ½-cup custard cups or ramekins. Place the cups in a baking pan and add hot water to reach halfway up the sides of the cups. Lay a piece of aluminum foil loosely on top of the cups.

Bake until just set but the centers still move slightly when the cups are shaken, 30 to 35 minutes. Remove from the oven and carefully remove the cups from the water bath. Let cool and cover the cups with plastic wrap. Refrigerate for at least 2 hours before serving. Garnish with whipped cream flavored with orange liqueur, brandy, or both.

SUMMER
CELEBRATION
ON THE LAWN

When Keith and Jon Meacham first married, they lived in Manhattan, in an apartment so small they slept on a Murphy bed. But as their family grew, so did their abodes—and Keith's now considerable entertaining skills expanded along with each space. Like me, Keith was born in the Mississippi Delta. She learned early on to dazzle the Yankees by simply making the stuff we know best, from pimento cheese sandwiches and ham biscuits to squash casseroles and rare beef tenderloin with warm yeast rolls. By the time the Meachams reached their last perch before decamping to Nashville, their annual holiday shindig was one of the city's most sought-after invitations.

Before I sold my own New York apartment, Keith and I plotted many a party together, including a huge bash to mark Jon's thirtieth birthday (attended by his then boss Katharine Graham and so jam-packed that people were hanging off the library ladder) and another, in honor of my father during the 2004 Republican convention, that the late, great Johnny Apple wrote up in the *New York Times.* There were smaller gatherings, too, of course, including the almost weekly dinners at my place on Saturday nights, after Jon, then the editor in chief of *Newsweek*, put the magazine to bed. For these, he would phone in requests: "Make that cheese thing with the vegetables," he'd say, in an effort to describe my Mexican corn bread.

Jon, now a Pulitzer Prize–winning author, was slightly more on point when he dubbed Keith's and my entertaining confabs the Crabmeat Caucus, and it's true that we might like the planning at least as much as the parties. We still meet, though now it's at the Meachams' gracious Georgian house in the Belle Meade section of Nashville. Going there is like going home, and not just because Keith and Jon are among my closest friends and their middle child, Mary, is my goddaughter. My mother and my aunt and all their cousins grew up in houses only blocks away, and I spent most of every summer in Nashville with my grandparents and my own cousins, who still live there.

I still return every chance I get, and I have to say that the new headquarters of the caucus—

Keith's comfortable and well-appointed kitchen—is a huge step above the cramped galley-style spaces we worked out of in New York. It was there in Keith's kitchen that we, along with our friend Diana Fisketjon, planned this particular event to honor Jack Spencer. Jack, an extraordinarily talented photographer whose show *Beyond the Surface* was opening at Nashville's Frist Center for the Visual Arts, had lots of out-of-town folks flying in for the occasion, and we wanted to entertain them in style with a country supper on the Meachams' lawn. Like Keith, Diana, and me, Jack is from Mississippi, so we pulled out all our old favorites, from fried chicken and a big platter of sliced tomatoes to Keith's mother's delicious blackberry cobbler.

Mary and her younger sister, Maggie, helped pass the hors d'oeuvres, and we served the supper buffet style from the dining room. Guests brought their plates outside and found their places at a long table set for twenty, where baskets of hot buttered biscuits greeted them. As an extra treat we put thin slices of Allan Benton's amazing country ham (see Sources, page 219) between each one (I love the salty ham with fried chicken), and gilded the lily by adding a smear of bourbon peach jam from my buddy Donald Link's Cochon Butcher, which just opened an outpost in Nashville (the original is in New Orleans). With dessert, we set out platters of sliced watermelon as a refreshing alternative (or addition) to the cobbler and poured healthy shots of Blanton's Single Barrel Bourbon for each guest.

There were plenty of toasts to Jack and his terrific show, which featured seventy images from his twenty-year-plus career. One of my favorites, the lovely *Isabel y Conjeo,* was used for the menu card, and I like to think that there were lots of similar subjects darting about in the darkness while we reveled in our dinner and the success of our friend.

The Menu

LAVENDER MINT LEMONADE
with Vodka

**BACON-WRAPPED
WATERMELON PICKLES**

OKRA FRITTERS
with Sriracha Mayonnaise

FRIED CHICKEN

**NANCY PETERKIN'S
SUMMER SQUASH CASSEROLE**

FIELD PEA & RICE SALAD

SLICED HEIRLOOM TOMATOES

BUTTERMILK BISCUITS
with Allan Benton's Country Ham

**MARY MACK'S
BLACKBERRY COBBLER**
with Bourbon Whipped Cream

Lavender Mint Lemonade
with Vodka

1 cup lavender sugar

8½ cups water

1 bunch mint, plus mint sprigs for garnish

Juice of **4** lemons, plus lemon slices for garnish

1¼ cups vodka

Fresh lavender sprigs for garnish

I use lavender simple syrup to flavor everything from whipped cream (excellent on chocolate desserts) to lemonade. Here, the syrup is also flavored with mint. Some lavender sugars still contain the dried flowers, which lend the syrup (and the drink) a lovely color.

Combine the lavender sugar and ½ cup of the water in a small saucepan. Bring to a boil over medium heat and cook just until the sugar has dissolved—do not let the mixture color. Remove from the heat and submerge the mint in the mixture.

When the mixture has cooled, strain it through a fine-mesh strainer into a large pitcher. (If your sugar contained dried lavender flowers, line the strainer with cheesecloth.) Add enough ice to fill the pitcher halfway, along with the remaining 8 cups water, the lemon juice, vodka, and ice, and stir. Pour into tall glasses and garnish with a lemon slice or two and a sprig each of lavender and mint.

Bacon-Wrapped Watermelon Pickles

Makes 20 hors d'oeuvres

One 10-ounce jar sweet pickled watermelon rind (I like Haddon House and Old South brands)

10 slices bacon, cut in half

This is the world's easiest hors d'oeuvre, and people go nuts over it. For the bacon, you need the cheap, relatively thin-sliced stuff like Oscar Mayer. As much as I love homemade watermelon pickles, for this a store-bought brand is better. The sticky-sweet syrup comes together with the salty, fatty bacon for a caramelized piece of perfection.

Preheat the oven to 375°F. Line a baking sheet with parchment paper and set aside.

Drain the watermelon pickles in a medium-mesh colander. Roll each half piece of bacon around a piece of pickled rind and secure with a toothpick.

Place the assembled pickles on the baking sheet. Bake until the bacon is well browned, about 20 minutes.

Okra Fritters
with Sriracha Mayonnaise

*Makes about
sixteen
2-inch fritters*

½ cup white cornmeal

½ cup all-purpose flour

1½ teaspoons salt, plus
more for sprinkling

1 teaspoon baking powder

1 large egg

½ cup buttermilk

½ cup finely chopped
sweet onion

2 cups thinly sliced okra

½ teaspoon freshly ground
black pepper

Vegetable oil for deep-
frying

Sriracha Mayonnaise

Makes 1 cup

1 large egg yolk, at room
temperature

2 teaspoons fresh lemon
juice

1 teaspoon Dijon mustard

¼ teaspoon salt

¾ cup vegetable or canola
oil

1½ teaspoons Sriracha
sauce

1 garlic clove, pressed

I adapted this recipe from one of my most treasured cookbooks, *The Gift of Southern Cooking* by Edna Lewis and Scott Peacock. When I serve the fritters as a side dish, I offer them up, piping hot, in a bread basket at the table, as though they were biscuits or cornbread. When I pass them as hors d'oeuvres, as at this dinner, I usually accompany them with a spicy Sriracha mayonnaise for dipping.

Place the cornmeal, flour, 1 teaspoon of the salt, and the baking powder in a large bowl and stir well. In a separate smaller bowl, whisk the egg and buttermilk together, then add the mixture to the dry ingredients and stir until just combined.

Wipe out the medium bowl and mix the onion and okra in it. Sprinkle with the remaining ½ teaspoon salt and the pepper, and toss to combine. Fold the vegetables into the batter.

Pour the vegetable oil into a heavy-bottomed skillet until it's 1 inch deep and heat until it's hot but not smoking. (If you have a deep-fry thermometer, it should register about 340°F.) Drop the batter by rounded tablespoons into the oil, being careful not to overcrowd. Fry until golden on one side, about 4 minutes, and then turn and repeat on the other side.

Remove the fritters from the skillet, drain on paper towels, and sprinkle with salt. You may keep them warm in a 200°F oven until all are done.

Sriracha Mayonnaise

Whisk together the egg yolk, lemon juice, mustard, and salt in a medium bowl until smooth. While still whisking, slowly dribble in the vegetable oil until the mayonnaise gets thick and the oil is easily incorporated. At this point, you can add the rest of the oil in a thin stream instead of drop by drop. If it gets too thick, add a teaspoon of water.

Whisk in the Sriracha and garlic and refrigerate, covered with plastic wrap, until ready to serve.

Fried Chicken

I f I'm making fried chicken to eat immediately, I use this same recipe, but I dry the chicken thoroughly after removing it from the buttermilk marinade. Instead of dredging, I place the flour mixture in a paper bag and toss the chicken pieces, a few at a time, until coated. Here, the chicken is dredged in the flour wet, which makes a thicker crust and chicken pieces that hold up far better over time. You will be happy to have enough left over to stick in the fridge for breakfast.

Put the chicken in a basin of cold water, soak for a few minutes to remove any traces of blood, and dry.

Stir together the buttermilk, hot sauce, and 2 tablespoons of the kosher salt in a large bowl or Dutch oven. Add the chicken, submerging the pieces. Cover with plastic wrap and refrigerate overnight.

Remove the chicken from the refrigerator and let stand at room temperature for about 1 hour. In a shallow dish, whisk together the flour, garlic powder, black pepper, cayenne, and the remaining 4 teaspoons kosher salt.

Remove the chicken from the marinade a few pieces at a time (do not shake off any excess). Dredge the chicken in the flour mixture, transfer to a baking sheet, and set aside.

Pour 2 inches of canola oil into a heavy-bottomed skillet and, over medium-high heat, bring to a temperature of 350°F. (Test the temperature with a candy or deep-fry thermometer, or dip a small corner of a chicken piece into the fat—if vigorous bubbling ensues, the temperature is right.) Slip the chicken into the oil, 3 or 4 pieces per batch, taking care not to crowd. Turn the heat down to medium and cover with a lid. Fry until golden brown on one side, 5 to 6 minutes for small pieces, 8 to 10 minutes for large. Remove the lid and turn the pieces with tongs. Fry, uncovered, until the second side is browned.

Using tongs, transfer the chicken to a wire rack set on a rimmed baking sheet and sprinkle with sea salt. Serve warm or at room temperature.

Serves 8 to 10

2 whole chickens, cut into 10 pieces each

4 cups buttermilk

½ cup Crystal hot sauce

2 tablespoons plus 4 teaspoons kosher salt

3½ cups all-purpose flour

2 tablespoons garlic powder

2 teaspoons freshly ground black pepper

1 teaspoon cayenne pepper

Canola, safflower, or vegetable oil for deep-frying

Flaky sea salt, such as Maldon

Nancy Peterkin's Summer Squash Casserole

Serves 8 to 10

8 tablespoons (1 stick) butter, plus more for greasing the baking dish

2 pounds yellow summer squash, scrubbed, trimmed, and cut into ½-inch slices

2 large garlic cloves, finely chopped

1 red bell pepper, seeded, cored, and chopped

1 jalapeño pepper, seeded and finely chopped

1 large onion, chopped

4 slices plain white bread, such as Pepperidge Farm, toasted

24 Ritz crackers, ground to fine crumbs in a food processor

½ pound sharp Cheddar cheese, grated

4 large eggs, beaten

½ cup heavy cream

1 teaspoon sugar

1 teaspoon salt

¼ teaspoon cayenne pepper

'm pretty sure I've never met a squash casserole I didn't love, and this one from my friend Nancy Peterkin, a justifiably renowned Houston hostess and terrific cook, is a particular favorite. It's crazy rich, but sharply flavorful, and is the perfect add-on to the other components of this dinner, which seem to demand something as luxuriously hot and cheesy. If you want a little more heat, add one or two more chopped jalapeños—this dish can take it.

Preheat the oven to 350°F. Butter a 2½-quart baking dish and set aside.

Place the squash slices in the bowl of a food processor fitted with a metal blade and pulse a couple of times so that the squash is chopped fairly finely. You will likely have to do this in batches.

Melt 6 tablespoons of the butter in a large deep skillet over medium heat. Add the squash and sauté for 3 to 4 minutes. Stir in the garlic, bell pepper, jalapeño, and onion. When the vegetables are tender, about 10 minutes more. Remove the skillet from the heat.

Meanwhile, crumb the toasted white bread (but not too finely) in the bowl of the food processor. Melt the remaining 2 tablespoons butter in a small saucepan and toss with the crumbs.

In a large bowl, place the squash mixture, cracker crumbs, and Cheddar and mix well. Stir in the beaten eggs, cream, sugar, salt, and cayenne. Blend well and pour into the prepared baking dish. Top with the buttered bread crumbs and bake for 40 minutes, until the crumbs are golden brown.

Field Pea & Rice Salad

2 pounds fresh field peas

1 smoked ham hock

2 white onions, halved

3 bay leaves

3 thyme sprigs

3 dried red chile peppers

2 teaspoons salt

6 bacon slices

2 celery stalks, chopped

1 green pepper, chopped

1 sweet onion, such as
  Vidalia, chopped

4 garlic cloves, chopped

2 tablespoons olive oil

1 pound andouille sausage,
  cut into ¼-inch dice

2 cups Uncle Ben's Original
  Converted rice

1 bunch scallions, thinly
  sliced, including about
  1 inch green stems

¼ cup finely chopped
  Italian parsley leaves

FOR THE VINAIGRETTE

¼ teaspoon salt

Freshly ground black
  pepper

1 generous teaspoon Dijon
  mustard

1½ tablespoons sherry
  vinegar

6 tablespoons extra-virgin
  olive oil

Hot sauce for serving

've rarely met a field pea and rice combo I didn't like, but in the summer I find those versions that are cooked forever with a ham hock (or sausage, or both) a tad too oppressive (and mushy) for the weather. This salad can be served cold or at room temperature, but its main advantage is that it has all the flavor imparted by the pork without the long cooking. Instead, it's layered in: The vegetables are sautéed in bacon grease, but not for so long that they lose their crunch; the peas cook only a short time with the ham hock, but the rice gets cooked in the same stock. For good measure, spicy andouille bits are tossed in, and a sharpish vinaigrette lightly binds everything together. Purple hull peas and crowder peas are especially good in this dish, but I usually use a mix of whatever is available at the farmers' market. Once, I even found fresh red beans for a decidedly lighter take on red beans and rice.

Place the peas in a colander and pick through, discarding any debris or beans that are shriveled or broken. Rinse in cold water.

Place the peas, ham hock, onion halves, bay leaves, thyme, chile peppers, and salt in a large pot and cover with water. Bring to a boil over high heat, skimming off the foam that collects on the surface. Reduce the heat and cook at a gentle simmer until the peas are tender but not too soft, stirring and skimming occasionally. The cooking time will vary—I'd start checking at 30 minutes. Strain the peas over another pot, reserving the broth and discarding the ham hock and seasonings.

While the peas are cooking, fry the bacon in a large skillet until at least 2 tablespoons of grease have been rendered. Remove the bacon from the skillet (and discard or eat!). Add the celery, green pepper, sweet onion, and garlic and stir, scraping up any leftover bacon brown bits. Sauté over medium-low heat for about 4 minutes, until the vegetables are just barely soft, and set aside.

In another skillet, heat the olive oil over medium heat. Add the andouille and cook, stirring occasionally, until browned and slightly caramelized, 5 or 6 minutes. Add the sausage to the vegetable mixture.

Place the rice and 4½ cups of the strained broth in a large pot, bring to a boil over high heat, cover, and simmer until the rice is done, about 20 minutes.

TO MAKE THE VINAIGRETTE

Combine the salt, pepper to taste, mustard, and vinegar in a small bowl and mix together with a small whisk. Whisk in the olive oil and set aside.

TO ASSEMBLE THE DISH

Fluff the rice when it is done and allow it to cool slightly. In a large bowl, combine the strained peas with the rice and the vegetable/andouille mixture and toss with the vinaigrette. Add the scallions and parsley, toss again, and taste for seasonings. Serve with hot sauce on the side.

Mary Mack's Blackberry Cobbler

I usually make my cobblers with shortbread biscuits on top, so when Keith made her mother's version with a crust, complete with crust "dumplings," it was a revelation. The pastry absorbs the delicious juices, and the grated lemon zest here is key. We served this with shots of Blanton's Single Barrel Bourbon, which we also used to flavor the accompanying whipped cream. The combination of the lemony, syrupy berries is somehow a perfect match with the sweet citrus and vanilla notes of the Blanton's. Also, you can certainly use other berries or peaches or both in this recipe, but I'm pretty wedded to the blackberry/lemon zest pair-up here.

Place the flour, salt, and shortening in the bowl of a food processor, and pulse until the mixture resembles small peas. (You can also do this in a mixing bowl with a pastry blender or a pair of forks.) Add about half of the ice water and pulse until the mixture comes together. If it's still crumbly, add the rest of the water, but be super careful not to overblend.

Remove the dough to a floured surface. Gather up about a quarter of the mixture and shape quickly into a small round. Shape the remaining mixture into a slightly bigger round, and wrap both in plastic wrap. Refrigerate for 30 minutes.

TO PREPARE THE COBBLER

Preheat oven to 350°F.

Mix the berries, sugar, and flour in a large bowl. Toss in the vanilla, lemon zest, and lemon juice.

Remove the small pastry round from the refrigerator and cut the dough into ½-inch-wide strips, about 2 inches long. Toss with the berries. Place the berry mixture in a 9 by 13-inch baking dish (or an oval one of approximate dimensions). Dot with the butter.

Remove the remaining pastry round from the refrigerator and place it on a floured surface. Roll it out into a rectangle large enough to cover the baking dish. Place the sheet on top of the berry mixture, tuck in the edges, and cut steam vents in a decorative pattern.

Place the baking dish on a baking sheet to catch any overflowing juices. Bake for 45 minutes to 1 hour, until the cobbler is bubbly and the crust is golden. Serve warm with whipped cream or ice cream.

Serves 8 to 10

FOR THE CRUST

2 cups sifted all-purpose flour

1½ teaspoons salt

¾ cup Crisco shortening, chilled

¼ cup ice water

FOR THE FILLING

4 cups blackberries

1½ cups sugar (or less if berries are very sweet)

1 tablespoon all-purpose flour

1 teaspoon pure vanilla extract

Grated zest and juice of 1 lemon

4 tablespoons (½ stick) salted butter, cut into thin slices

SUMMERTIME BLUES

- **Fried Chicken**
Eden Brent

- **Summertime**
Billie Holiday & Her Orchestra

- **Let's Boogie Woogie**
Eden Brent

- **Mary Jane's Last Dance**
Tom Petty & the Heartbreakers

- **I'm Just a Prisoner**
Candi Staton

- **Heart on a String**
Jason Isbell & The 400 Unit

- **In the Midnight Hour**
Wilson Pickett

- **Jigsaw Heart**
Eden Brent

- **Summertime**
Janis Joplin

- **Hurricanes & Hand Grenades**
Jason Isbell

- **Mississippi Number One**
Eden Brent

- **Call Me**
St. Paul & The Broken Bones

- **Walking the Dog**
*Bonnie Raitt &
Weepin' Willie Robinson*

For Jack's party, we hired Eden Brent, my dear friend and fellow Mississippi Deltan, to entertain us with her passion-filled blend of blues, jazz, and soul. Eden studied classical music at the University of North Texas College of Music, but she got her education during a sixteen-year stint with Abie "Boogaloo" Ames, a rollicking blues pianist from our hometown who dubbed her "Little Boogaloo." A three–time Blues Music Award winner, she's

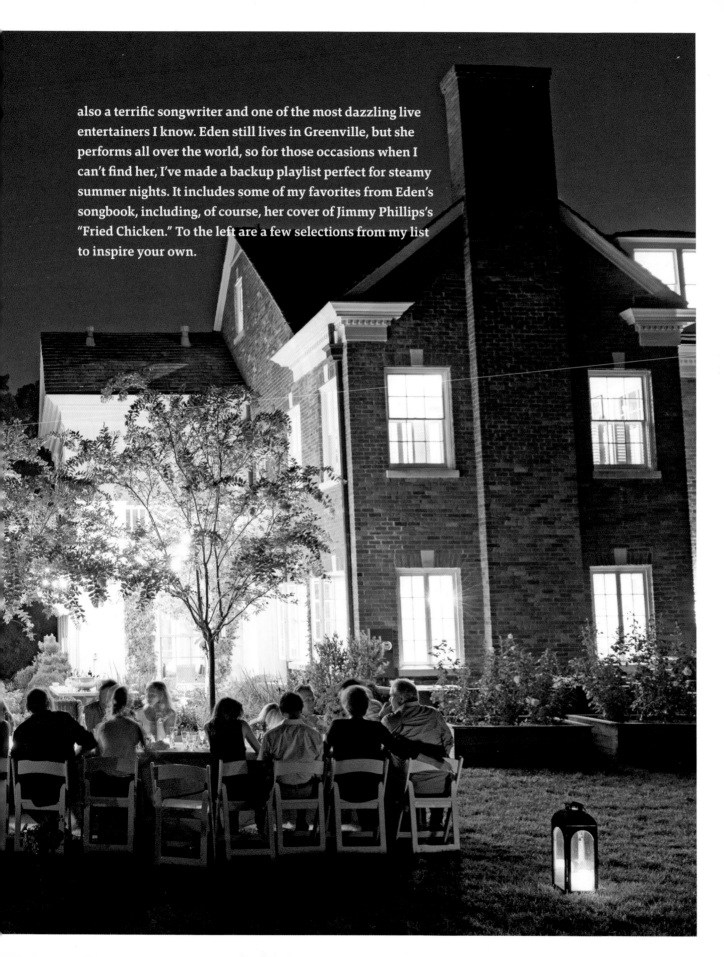

also a terrific songwriter and one of the most dazzling live entertainers I know. Eden still lives in Greenville, but she performs all over the world, so for those occasions when I can't find her, I've made a backup playlist perfect for steamy summer nights. It includes some of my favorites from Eden's songbook, including, of course, her cover of Jimmy Phillips's "Fried Chicken." To the left are a few selections from my list to inspire your own.

Champagne loves two things in food: salt & fat

A NOTE ON BISCUITS & FRIED CHICKEN

I can make biscuits and I can fry chicken, but I rarely do either—especially not for a party of this size (twenty people). There are plenty of folks who do both at least as well as or far better than I. And they're all just a car ride, click, or phone call away.

At our party for Jack, we served Mary B's Biscuits, a Pensacola, Florida–based brand that comes in six varieties, including bite-size tea buttermilk, which are great for hors d'oeuvres. They're sold in handy Ziploc-like bags in the freezer sections of Walmarts and supermarkets across the country. Keith loves Mary B's biscuits, while I'm a longtime Marshall's girl. I love the old-fashioned tin baking tray they come in. If you can't find them in supermarkets between Texas and Virginia, you can order them delivered to your door from Sister Schuberts (see Sources, page 219), where I also get my yeast rolls. The trick is to brush melted butter on the tops of any of these biscuits before baking. When they're done, split them apart and brush the insides with plenty more butter.

As for the chicken, I'm not ashamed to admit that it came from the Piggly Wiggly supermarket on Columbia Avenue in Franklin, Tennessee, just outside of Nashville. Most Southerners know that supermarket (and even gas station) chicken can be a good thing indeed—Diana sussed out this particular spot, near where she and her husband, Gary, own a home, as having some talented folks on staff doing the frying and seasoning. (Rouses and Publix are two other chains that are usually dependable.)

Diana says she always tells them to leave the boxes open so that the chicken doesn't steam, and offers a further helpful note: "One thing I do before serving the chicken is lay it out, piece by piece, on an oven wire rack with a pan on the rack below to collect the grease. Let it sit in a warm oven, 275°F, for about an hour. You'll be surprised at the oil rendered by this process. Your chicken will be even better after this is done, whether served hot or cold."

I'd be remiss here if I didn't give a nod to the Colonel, who put takeout chicken on the map (who does not secretly love a bucket of KFC?), and to Popeyes, which I served at dinner parties in Manhattan to great acclaim. The following is an entirely subjective short list of chicken sources that will keep you from standing over a hot stove for hours on end.

PRINCE'S HOT CHICKEN, NASHVILLE, TENNESSEE

Nashville is the hot chicken capital of the country (the city now has more than a dozen spots that specialize in it, as well as a Music City Hot Chicken Festival) but Prince's, which won the James Beard Foundation's America's Classics Award in 2013, is where it all started. The legend is that one of the many girlfriends of founding owner Thornton Prince got sick of his late-night carousing and gave his Sunday morning chicken an overdose of cayenne pepper. Thornton must have been made of some stern stuff—not only did he like it, he perfected the process and started selling it in the 1930s. Today, his great-niece, André Prince Jeffries, continues the tradition, selling mild, hot, and extra hot, accompanied by dill pickles and slices of white bread. (The mild, I hasten to add, is as powerful as a normal human will want to go.) These days, "hot chicken" has become a thing—you can find it on swanky menus across the country—but Prince's is the original deal.

McHARDY'S CHICKEN AND FIXIN', NEW ORLEANS, LOUISIANA

When I'm home in New Orleans, this Seventh Ward institution is my go-to spot. Highly seasoned and perfectly salted, this chicken is always fresh, light, and exceptionally crispy. It's also the best bargain in town, and they pack the chicken wisely—in white cardboard pastry boxes with butcher paper between the layers. Give McHardy's a pickup time and they'll cook chicken to order just beforehand.

GUS'S WORLD FAMOUS FRIED CHICKEN, MEMPHIS, TENNESSEE, AND BEYOND

Opened more than sixty years go in Mason, Tennessee, Gus's now has eleven locations, including two in Memphis, with plans to expand in cities as far flung as Los Angeles and Detroit. The good news is that no matter where you buy it, the chicken retains its handmade quality and spicy edge.

BIRDS AND BUBBLES

When I was picking out wine to go with our fried chicken, my extremely knowledgeable pal Jim Yonkus, co-owner of Keife & Co. in New Orleans (see Sources, page 219), steered me straight to the Champagne section, specifically to Pierre Brigandat & Fils Brut Tradition NV. Made in the southernmost extremities of Champagne with 100 percent pinot noir grapes, it has enough heartiness and rich round fruit—plus a little toast and butter—to make it a perfect match. "This wine," says Jim, "is fried chicken juice."

Seth Box, the director of education for Moët-Hennessy, says he thinks most bubbly would fit that description: "Champagne loves two things in food: salt and fat" (which means it's tailor-made for pretty much everything else on this menu, from the ham biscuits to the squash casserole). Box, too, is crazy for the "richness and texture of fried chicken" with the "crispness and acidity of the Champagne." The acidity is indeed key—it's the reason why so many chicken joints add a pile of hamburger dills to their chicken boxes.

Since this dinner, the affordable Brigandat has become one of my favorite Champagnes. Other good fried chicken choices would be the Crémant de Bourgogne Blanc from Domaine Brigand G. (made from pinot noir and chardonnay grapes and possessed of a lovely biscuity nose) or even a super affordable cava from Spain. The main thing is the bubbles.

DINNER ON THE HALF SHELL

I swear I think I owe the evolution of this menu to my friend Christopher Gow and his vast offerings of silvered seashells at least as much as I do to the actual shellfish. I began collecting Christopher's magical wares in the very early 1990s, when his business was called Ruzzetti and Gow and operated out of a third-floor walk-up in Manhattan's dingy West 30s. These days his partner is Jamie Creel and their shop (now Creel and Gow, see Sources, page 218) on East 70th Street is a dazzling cabinet of curiosities, but those shells are still as popular as ever. My own collection includes starfish and sea urchin candleholders, ingenious cockleshell place-card holders, burgus shell salts, and lots more specimens to sprinkle about the table.

Such gorgeous props demand a menu like this one, and to complete the look, I encrusted vases (with the help of a glue gun) with natural shells, inspired by an ancient Ralph Lauren lamp that was a gift from my generous friend Bobby Harling. This particular dinner took place in my mother's lovely dining room, and, as luck would have it, her silver pattern is Fiddle, Thread, and Shell. For the hors d'oeuvres course, we let guests help themselves to both fried and baked oysters from our combined collections of oyster plates on the sideboard. The theme continued on the outside bar, where a giant clamshell served as a wine cooler and an enormous shell-encrusted bowl (another gift from Bobby) served as a receptacle for the cocktail's citrus.

My favorite wine with oysters is always a Muscadet. We served a Chablis with the soup course. The vivid acidity of the Grüner Veltliner from Austria's Weingut Knoll (one of the most versatile wines ever) made it the perfect match for the shrimp, which contains a healthy dose of curry.

The Menu

SOUTHSIDE COCKTAILS

OYSTERS ROCKEFELLER

FRIED OYSTERS
with Fennel Aioli

GREEN GODDESS SOUP
with Jumbo Lump Crabmeat

SHRIMP MALACCA
with Rice

JUSTINE'S
PINEAPPLE MINT
ICE CREAM

The Southside

Serves 1

8 mint leaves, plus 1 mint sprig for garnish

1 piece lemon zest, about 1 inch long by ½ inch wide

3 ounces gin

1 ounce Simple Syrup

1½ ounces fresh lemon juice, plus 2 lemon slices for garnish

¾ ounce club soda or Champagne

The Southside, like the gin and tonic, is one of those cocktails that heralds warm weather. There are warring stories over its Prohibition-era invention: It was created at the Southside Sportsmen's Club on Long Island, or at Manhattan's "21" Club while it was still a speakeasy, or on Chicago's South Side (by gangsters who wanted to mask the taste of inferior gin). Wherever, it's differentiated from a Tom Collins by the refreshing addition of mint, and more recent variations include adding a touch of bitters {Fee Brothers Old Fashion Aromatic Bitters (see Sources, page 219) go well with the gin's complex flavors} and replacing the club soda with Champagne for a Southside Royale (Hendrick's gin is especially nice for this combo).

Place the mint leaves and lemon zest at the bottom of a cocktail shaker and crush with the back of a spoon or a muddler to release their essential oils. Add the gin, simple syrup, and lemon juice and shake well. Pour into a goblet or a collins glass filled with ice, top with the club soda, and garnish with a mint sprig and lemon slices.

NOTE: *For a pitcher of Southsides, do the math according to how many you want to serve, and muddle the citrus and mint at the bottom of a pitcher. Add the gin, simple syrup, and lemon juice and stir vigorously until blended. Top with the club soda.*

Makes 2 cups

1 cup sugar

1 cup water

Simple Syrup

In a medium saucepan, combine the sugar and water. Bring to a boil over high heat. Reduce the heat and simmer, stirring, for 2 to 3 minutes, until the sugar has completely dissolved. Remove from the heat immediately and allow to cool before serving. The syrup may be refrigerated in a glass jar for up to 1 month.

Oysters Rockefeller

This dish was invented in 1899 at New Orleans's Antoine's Restaurant, which, understandably, has never given out the recipe. In an effort to re-create it, too many cooks mistake the green stuff for spinach, but spinach-topped oysters are correctly called oysters Florentine. In all my years of research, the recipe I like best is one adapted from *James Beard's New Fish Cookery*, an indispensable guide to cooking all things seafood.

Preheat the oven to 475°F.

Melt 3 tablespoons of the butter in a large skillet over medium-high heat. Add the chopped fennel and fennel greens, scallions, celery, chervil, and parsley and sauté for 3 minutes, or until tender. Add the watercress and cook for 2 minutes, or until just wilted.

Place the green vegetable mixture in the bowl of a food processor. Cut 3 tablespoons of the remaining butter into pieces and add it to the mixture, along with 2 tablespoons of the bread crumbs, the Pernod, salt, black pepper, and cayenne. Process for 1 minute.

Arrange the oysters on a bed of rock salt in a shallow pan. Top each oyster with enough of the pureed mixture to cover, about 2 teaspoons, depending on the size of the oyster.

In a small skillet, melt the remaining 2 tablespoons butter over medium-high heat and sauté the remaining 4 tablespoons bread crumbs until just golden, 1 to 2 minutes. Sprinkle each oyster with a pinch of the crumbs. Bake for 6 to 8 minutes, until the oysters are hot and plumped.

Place the oysters on oyster plates or arrange them on a bed of rock salt on a serving tray or platter. Set out small plates and oyster forks so that guests can help themselves to 1 or 2 as an hors d'oeuvre, or, as a first course, serve 6 on a plate.

Serves 4 as a first course, or 6 to 8 as hors d'oeuvres

8 tablespoons (1 stick) butter

¼ cup chopped trimmed fennel bulb, plus **1** tablespoon chopped fennel greens

2 tablespoons chopped scallions

2 tablespoons chopped celery

1 tablespoon chopped chervil leaves

¼ cup chopped Italian parsley leaves

1 cup trimmed watercress, rinsed and dried

6 tablespoons bread crumbs

1 tablespoon Pernod

½ teaspoon salt

¼ teaspoon freshly ground black pepper

Pinch of cayenne pepper

2 dozen oysters on the half shell

Rock salt

Fried Oysters with Fennel Aioli

My friend the late Michael Cordes introduced me to this seriously tasty aioli, which he served with poached shrimp. Here, I use it as a dip for fried oysters. More unexpected than the typical tartar sauce, it has the same licorice-like flavor of Oysters Rockefeller (page 79), which makes it fun to serve alongside them.

Drain the oysters. Spread the cornmeal on a baking sheet and dredge the oyster in it, one at a time. Place the oysters in a colander, shaking off any excess cornmeal.

Heat the vegetable oil in a deep skillet over medium-high heat until it reaches 350°F. (You can also check the temperature by sprinkling some of the cornmeal into the oil. If it spins and dances, the oil should be ready.) Gently drop an oyster into the hot oil. If it doesn't rise to the top, wait a minute or two and try again. If it does, add 3 or 4 more oysters, being careful not to crowd the pan. When the oysters are a light brown, remove them with a slotted spoon to paper towels to drain.

Place the oysters on oyster plates or a small platter and serve with the fennel aioli on the side for dipping. You could also pass them on a platter with a small bowl of the aioli in the center.

Fennel Aioli

Heat 3 tablespoons of the olive oil in a skillet over medium heat. Add the fennel slices, vinegar, and fennel seeds and sauté for 10 minutes, stirring often. Add half the garlic slices and the remaining 1½ cups oil. Reduce the heat to low, cover, and cook until the fennel is tender, stirring occasionally, about 35 minutes.

With a slotted spoon, remove the fennel and garlic to the bowl of a food processor, reserving the oil. (Do not use a blender.) Add the remaining garlic slices to the food processor. Process for a few seconds and, with the machine running, add the egg yolks, one at a time. Process until smooth. While the machine is still running, add the oil from the fennel mixture in a slow, steady stream, until the mixture is emulsified. Season with salt and white pepper.

NOTE: *This aioli is also terrific with the aforementioned poached shrimp or pretty much any grilled or poached white fish.*

*Serves 6 to 8
as hors d'oeuvres*

1 pint fresh shucked oysters

1½ cups white cornmeal or unseasoned Zatarain's Fish Fri

4 cups vegetable oil for deep-frying

Fennel Aoli for serving

*Makes about
2½ cups*

1½ cups plus 3 tablespoons extra-virgin olive oil

2 medium fennel bulbs, trimmed and sliced

1 tablespoon white wine vinegar

1½ teaspoons fennel seeds, chopped

3 garlic cloves, sliced

3 large egg yolks

Salt and freshly ground white pepper

Green Goddess Soup
with Jumbo Lump Crabmeat

At her popular Los Angeles dinner parties, my good friend Suzanne Rheinstein, an interior designer and New Orleans native, often serves a first course consisting of a generous scoop of jumbo lump blue crab napped with green goddess dressing. The pale green-and-white color combo is gorgeous, and the Californians, used to flaky Dungeness crab, always swoon. The first time I tasted the combo, I was struck not by the crab (which I'm blessedly used to) but by how perfect the tart, herby dressing was with the lush crabmeat. I now serve what I think of as "Suzanne's Green Goddess Crabmeat" a lot, but for this dinner, which features an embarrassment of shellfish riches, an entire serving of crab would be too much. Instead, I inverted the dish by making a soup out of green goddess ingredients and using a few lumps of crab as garnish only. Even without the crab, the soup (inspired by a recipe from another pal, Nora Etheridge) is pretty great.

Place the cucumber, avocado, scallions, parsley, tarragon leaves, and chopped chives in the bowl of a food processor. Process for about 10 seconds. Add the chicken stock, sour cream, lemon juice, salt, and cayenne. Process for another 10 seconds, or until the mixture is smooth and well blended.

Pour the soup into a large bowl, cover with plastic wrap, and chill for at least 2 hours. When ready to serve, ladle into soup bowls or plates, garnish with a couple of lumps of the crabmeat, and sprinkle with the minced tarragon and minced chives.

NOTE: *I like to serve this soup accompanied by thin slices of baguette brushed with melted butter, toasted, and sprinkled with sea salt. Make enough to offer with the next course, Shrimp Malacca (page 85), as well.*

*Serves 8
as a first course*

1 medium cucumber, peeled, seeded, and roughly chopped

1 ripe medium avocado, peeled, pitted, and quartered

6 scallions, including about 1 inch of the green stem, roughly chopped (about 1 cup)

¼ cup Italian parsley leaves, roughly chopped

1 tablespoon tarragon leaves, plus 1 tablespoon minced for garnish

1 tablespoon chives, roughly chopped, plus 1 tablespoon minced for garnish

1 cup unsalted chicken stock

1 cup sour cream

3 tablespoons fresh lemon juice

1 teaspoon salt

Pinch of cayenne pepper

1 pound jumbo lump crabmeat

Shrimp Malacca
with Rice

I found this recipe by Maurice Moore-Betty in a late 1970s issue of *House & Garden* while I was still in college, and I've been making it ever since. Moore-Betty was an Irish-born author, cooking teacher, and all-around lovely man who also advised many a prominent Manhattan hostess. This dish is essentially shrimp Creole with the addition of curry powder, which elevates it by a surprising degree. Serve over rice, accompanied by a simple green salad.

Heat the vegetable oil over medium heat in a large heavy saucepan. Add the onions, bell pepper, and celery and cook until soft, stirring occasionally.

Add the tomatoes, tomato puree, cayenne, basil, garlic, bay leaves, and salt and black pepper to taste. Bring to a boil over high heat and add the curry powder. Turn down the heat and simmer the mixture, covered, for about 25 minutes. If the sauce seems too thick, thin it with a little seafood stock or water. Add the shrimp and simmer for about 10 minutes, until just cooked through. Remove the bay leaves.

Serve over cooked white rice (I love Uncle Ben's Original Converted rice).

Serves 8

⅓ cup vegetable or canola oil

2 medium yellow onions, finely diced

1 large green bell pepper, seeded, stemmed, and finely diced

2 celery stalks, peeled and diced (about ½ cup)

One 16-ounce can whole peeled Italian plum tomatoes

1 cup tomato puree

Generous pinch of cayenne pepper

Generous pinch of dried basil

2 garlic cloves, mashed with 1 teaspoon kosher salt

2 bay leaves

Salt and freshly ground black pepper

2 tablespoons curry powder

3 pounds (36 to 40 count) shrimp, peeled

Boxed or canned seafood stock, if needed, or use Homemade Shrimp Stock (page 22)

Cooked white rice for serving

Justine's Pineapple Mint Ice Cream

Makes about 3 quarts, or serves 10 to 12

1¼ cups sugar

1¼ cups water

2 cups lightly packed mint leaves

½ cup light corn syrup

2 cups canned crushed pineapple in its own juice

1½ cups canned pineapple juice

2 cups whole milk

2 cups heavy cream

¼ cup white crème de menthe

1 cup fresh lemon juice

Shortbread cookies for garninsh

Justine's, the Memphis restaurant housed in an ivy-covered nineteenth-century mansion on the banks of the Mississippi River, was the first "fine dining" restaurant in which I ever ate. Long before anyone had ever heard the phrase "farm to table," the garden at Justine's provided both fresh produce and old roses, and the food was so good we made the two-and-a-half-hour trek north from Greenville with astonishing frequency. Most famous for the buttery crabmeat Justine, the restaurant always featured at least one or two homemade ice creams for dessert, often served in scoops piled high in silver bowls on the antique sideboards. This one is easy, refreshing, and echoes the flavors of the Southside cocktail we started off with.

Combine the sugar and water in a medium saucepan and bring to a boil over medium-high heat cooking until the sugar has dissolved. Boil without stirring for about 10 minutes, until it reaches the soft-ball stage (234° to 240°F on a candy thermometer), when a drop forms a soft ball in a cup of cold water. Stir in the mint and simmer over medium heat for 10 minutes more. Remove from the heat and let cool.

Pour the mint syrup into a blender and puree. Strain into a large bowl. Stir in the corn syrup.

Rinse the blender, add the pineapple and pineapple juice, and puree. Add the pineapple pureé to the mint syrup mixture along with the milk, cream, crème de menthe, and lemon juice.

Chill for at least 4 hours or overnight (in a pinch, I put it in the freezer for an hour). Transfer the chilled mixture to an ice cream maker and freeze according to the manufacturer's directions.

Scrape the ice cream into a large bowl. Cover with plastic wrap and place in the freezer until ready to serve. When ready to serve, scoop into dessert bowls or cups and garnish with shortbread cookies.

TOMATOPALOOZA

My friends Ben and Libby Page are the owners of Brookside, which is (to use one of my father's favorite expressions) "a little piece of paradise" located in the rolling hills of Giles County, Tennessee. The house, a mid-nineteenth-century Greek Revival situated on fifty-four glorious acres, is named after the nearby Italianate Revival structure where Libby's grandmother grew up. Ben, a landscape architect based in Nashville, where he and Libby keep their primary home, designed its vegetable and cutting gardens, as well as a gorgeous boxwood parterre filled with lilies and grasses, just behind a picture-perfect red barn.

It's all bounded by the original stone wall Ben has painstakingly restored, and in the summer months, the cutting garden is a riot of zinnias, enormous marigolds, and celosia. The vegetable garden is home to all manner of goodness, including sweet corn, okra, Kentucky Wonder and pole beans, cucumbers, and a vast collection of heirloom tomatoes. Libby is an event planner and a terrific cook who puts all that produce to very good use. The Pages' festive Saturday night feasts are always preceded by a trip up to the ridge on Ben's John Deere Gator, where guests watch the sunset with cocktails in hand.

Libby and I have been friends since childhood (our great-grandfathers founded an insurance company together), and Ben designed my former garden in New Orleans. I love them and I love Brookside, so when I concocted the idea of a multicourse tomato-based dinner, I could think of no better place.

I should add here that I'm a lifelong tomato fanatic—when other kids were toting peanut butter and jelly sandwiches to school in their lunch boxes and bags, I made like one of my favorite literary heroines, Harriet the Spy, and invariably insisted on tomato. But folks wishing for a tiny bit more variety could easily use one or two of the courses featured here in a less tomato-centric menu. I did manage to introduce a few other items—fig halves wrapped in serrano ham that we included as an hors d'oeuvre, for example, and the shortcakes piled with peach slices poached in red wine. Still, I made sure that most of the main ingredients were in pretty shades of pink and red. As it happens, French rosé wines pair perfectly with the various dishes on offer, so our theme was complete, aided, as well, by Ben's spectacular zinnias on the table. Now we have an annual tradition, and I'm so glad, because there is no more fitting—or gorgeous—setting in which to celebrate my favorite among all of summer's bounty.

A postscript: On the morning after what has inevitably become known as Tomatopalooza, Libby made us BLTs with locally cured bacon and some of the bread left over from the previous evening's bruschetta. The tomatoes were already warm from the morning sun, and there on the side was the corn relish she puts up every year. Heaven.

A NOTE ON THE TABLE SETTING

I love red, white, and blue together any time, but this particular combination would make for a very chic Memorial Day or Fourth of July gathering. Here, though, both the menu and the "props" are pretty multicultural. The tablecloth is made of a woven ticking made by my friend, the Massachusetts-based fabric designer Peter Fasano, and the accompanying napkins are vintage French raw linen dishtowels (which means they have the ample size I love). The plates are part of a set of antique English Blue Willow china, a gift from my equally porcelain-obsessed pal Robert Harling. I often mix the real deal with cheap knock-off pieces that I pick up in various Chinatowns, and here I mixed them with inexpensive blue glass goblets and Libby's fine family silver. I hauled those French rush-bottomed chairs all the way from New Orleans in a rented Yukon. I had to—I knew they'd look great with the barn. In the end, the mix of provenances and high-and-low elements is fun and completely fitting for a menu that runs the gamut from an Italian-inspired bruschetta and a Spanish soup to a French soufflé and all-American shortcake.

The Menu

PINK PERFECTION

BRUSCHETTA
with Fig Relish & Buratta

GAZPACHO
with Tomato Sherbet

ZUCCHINI PUDDING SOUFFLÉS
with Creamy Tomato Sauce

TOMATO TARTE TATIN

SLICED CHICKEN BREAST
with Tomato Vinaigrette

ALMOND BUTTERMILK SHORTCAKES
*with Peaches Poached in Red Wine
and White Chocolate
Whipped Cream*

YOU SAY TOMATO, I SAY ROSÉ

Tomatoes and rosés have always been the twin totems of summer to me. Not only is the wine's color made for our tomato lovefest, so, as it happens, is the taste. Herewith, a rundown of the pairings:

AMEZTOI TXAKOLINA RUBENTIS

Both the rosé and the white from this Basque country producer are among my favorite summer wines. Light, crisp, and mineraly, they're bottled with residual carbon, which provides their signature natural spritz. The vineyards are at the edge of the Atlantic Ocean, and you can practically taste the sea air with each sip (or gulp—this is a thirst-quenching wine). We drank the rosé with the hors d'oeuvres and kept at it through the first course. It was the perfect foil for the salty serrano ham that encased the figs, as well as for the rich burrata smearing the bruschetta. And, naturally, it was terrific with the gazpacho, as both the wine and the soup hail from roughly the same neck of the woods.

TIBOUREN CLOS CIBONNE ROSÉ

Tibouren is a rare local grape that grows in southern Provence, near Bandol, on land overlooking another body of water—this time, the Mediterranean. Fresh, vibrant, and eminently food friendly, it has a gorgeous pale orange color, a beautiful label, and the tiniest taste of sherry that I adore. The combination of fruit and salinity gives it both the balance and the backbone to stand up to the lemony, intensely tomatoey vinaigrette that accompanies the sliced chicken breast.

MAS CAL DEMOURA QU'ES AQUO

This rosé from one of the finest estates in the Languedoc is darker and richer than those of Provence, which means that it paired beautifully with the richest dish of the dinner—the cheesy zucchini puddings with tomato cream sauce.

DOMAINE TEMPIER BANDOL ROSÉ

No producer is more synonymous with rosé than Domaine Tempier. Owned by the iconic Peyraud family and championed by the likes of Richard Olney, Alice Waters, and Kermit Lynch, this age-worthy wine has a cult following for a reason. Here it was served with the tomato tarte tatin, the most provençal of the menu's dishes, but there is little (from a Thanksgiving turkey to a wintry beef daube) that it doesn't enhance.

Pink Perfection

Pink Perfection is the name of a much-loved camellia, but this drink comes pretty close to perfection in a glass. Unless you live near a juice bar that makes fresh, strained watermelon juice daily, I strongly recommend making the juice yourself. The "fresh" stuff sold in stores in plastic bottles is usually far too cloying, and besides, this is easy to do. And if you prefer vodka to rum, the drink works just as well.

Combine the rum, watermelon juice, lime juice, simple syrup, and some ice in a cocktail shaker and shake. Strain into a glass and garnish with an orange slice and a mint sprig.

NOTE: *You can also do the math on this and make up a whole pitcher of Pink Perfection if you're having a crowd. In that case, I'd mix it without ice, so as not to dilute the drink, and chill.*

Serves 1

¼ cup Orange-Infused Rum (recipe follows)
¾ cup Fresh Watermelon Juice (recipe follows)
1 tablespoon fresh lime juice
1 teaspoon Simple Syrup (page 78)
1 orange slice for garnish
1 mint sprig for garnish

Orange-Infused Rum

Cut the orange slices in half and place in a pitcher large enough to accommodate them and the rum. Pour the rum over the oranges and refrigerate overnight.

NOTE: *You'll have plenty of the infused rum left over. Strain the remaining infused rum into a mason jar and store indefinitely in the refrigerator.*

Makes 1 litter

2 large navel oranges, rinsed, dried cut into ¼-inch slices
1 liter white rum

Fresh Watermelon Juice

Set a fine-mesh strainer over a large bowl (I use a stockpot, especially when I double this recipe) and set aside.

Place the watermelon in a blender and blend until liquefied, about 1 minute. Pour through the strainer into the bowl and use a spatula to push the liquid through until only the pulp remains. Discard the pulp. You will have to do this in batches, but you should have about 6 cups watermelon juice when done. Chill until cold, or for up to 1 day.

Makes 6 cups

6 pounds seedless watermelon, rind removed, cut into 1-inch chunks (about 12 cups)

Bruschetta
with Fig Relish & Buratta

*Makes 16
hors d'oeuvres*

FOR THE FIG RELISH

3 large ripe Mission or
Brown Turkey figs or
20 Celestes, stemmed
and finely chopped

1 medium red onion, finely
chopped (about ½ cup)

1 serrano chile, stemmed,
seeded, and finely
chopped

½ cup mint leaves,
chopped

¼ cup fresh lime juice

1 tablespoon good-quality
balsamic vinegar

1 teaspoon salt

1 teaspoon freshly ground
black pepper

FOR THE BRUSCHETTA

8 slices sourdough bread,
about ¾ inch thick

Extra-virgin olive oil

One 8-ounce ball burrata
cheese

I adore bruschetta topped with chopped tomatoes (I mix mine with garlic, basil, and olive oil), but because we already have a plethora of tomatoes, I decided to go with my favorite summer relish, made with figs, instead. I adapted this recipe years ago from one created by my friend and fellow fig devotee Jeremiah Tower. In the early part of the summer, I use the Celeste or "sugar" figs that are so plentiful in the Southeast, but Mission and Brown Turkey do just as well. This recipe couldn't be easier. You'll likely have some relish left over, but you might want to double the recipe anyway—it's divine with grilled duck, pork chops, lamb, country ham, you name it.

TO MAKE THE FIG RELISH

Combine the figs, onion, chile, mint, lime juice, vinegar, salt, and pepper in a medium bowl and mix well. Let sit for at least 1 hour at room temperature, or cover and refrigerate for up to 4 days. When ready to serve, prepare the bruschetta.

TO MAKE THE BRUSCHETTA

Prepare a fire in a grill or preheat the broiler. Grill or broil the bread slices for about 30 seconds on each side, until crisp and golden. You want some grill marks or brown bits to appear, but be careful not to burn the slices. Brush one side of each slice with olive oil and, depending on its width, cut in half or into thirds. Top each piece with a slice of the burrata. It will be messy (that's the nature of burrata and its scrumptiousness) so you might have to spoon it from the round and spread it over the toast. Spoon the fig relish on top of the burrata and serve.

NOTE: *If a fat sourdough loaf or country round can't be found, use a baguette and double the number of slices.*

Gazpacho
with Tomato Sherbet

This dish has an inspirational history that winds from a country club in Nashville, Tennessee, to my friend Charlotte Moss's garden. Years ago, I wrote a piece in the *New York Times Magazine* about the "frozen tomato," an almost freakishly delicious tomato sherbet of a sort served at the Belle Meade Country Club, where my grandparents were members. Nora Ephron saw the recipe and wrote me a lovely, funny (of course) letter reporting that she'd added the frozen tomato to her heirloom tomato salad plate and that it was a huge hit at her Hamptons table. When Nora died, I decided to create a slightly less garish version (one without red food coloring or shredded pineapple—don't ask!) as a centerpiece to a tomato salad inspired by her, and then I included it in a *Wall Street Journal* column. Charlotte saw *that* recipe, made it for a dinner party, and very sweetly wrote about it in her blog—adding that she plopped scoops of the leftover tomato sherbet into bowls of gazpacho at lunch the next day. I tried the same thing almost immediately, and it turns out to be an inspired idea. This is an amazingly refreshing dish for a hot day. And I am grateful to both women for leading me to it.

Place the cucumbers, tomatoes, and bell peppers in the bowl of a food processor and add the lemon juice, vinegar, and olive oil. Process until just blended and still slightly chunky. Pour into a large bowl or soup tureen and stir in the garlic, parsley, salt, and black pepper. Cover and refrigerate for at least 1 but not more than 8 hours.

When ready to serve, pour the gazpacho into six bowls and top with a scoop of tomato sherbet and a basil sprig.

NOTE: *I am generally an onion fanatic, but I like the simplicity and sweetness of this soup without the onion just this once. The acidic balance is pretty close to perfect, but if you must, you can add 1 small sweet onion, coarsely chopped, to the mix before processing.*

Serves 6

3 large cucumbers, peeled, seeded, and roughly chopped

6 large ripe tomatoes, peeled, seeded, and roughly chopped

2 red bell peppers stemmed, seeded, and roughly chopped

2 teaspoons fresh lemon juice

2 teaspoons sherry vinegar

2 tablespoons extra-virgin olive oil

2 garlic cloves, crushed and finely chopped

3 tablespoons Italian parsley leaves, chopped

1 teaspoon salt

2 teaspoons freshly ground black pepper

Basil sprigs for garnish

Tomato Sherbet (recipe follows) for garnish

3 cups chopped, peeled, and seeded tomatoes

½ teaspoon salt, plus more for the tomatoes

Freshly ground white pepper

1 cup Hellmann's mayonnaise

1 tablespoon heavy cream

1 teaspoon sugar

Pinch of cayenne pepper

2 teaspoons fresh lemon juice

½ teaspoon Lea & Perrins Worcestershire sauce

Tomato Sherbet

Put the tomatoes in a heavy-bottomed saucepan and season them with a healthy pinch of salt and a few lashings of white pepper. Bring to a simmer and cook for 25 minutes, stirring occasionally and scraping the bottom of the pan.

Transfer the tomatoes to a blender or the bowl of a food processor and puree. Place 2½ cups of the puree in a medium bowl and chill in the freezer until ice-cold but not frozen. Return to the blender or food processor and add the remaining puree, the mayonnaise, cream, remaining ½ teaspoon salt, the cayenne, lemon juice, and Worcestershire sauce and blend thoroughly. Pour the mixture into an ice cream maker and freeze according to the manufacturer's instructions.

NOTE: *You may need to finish the sherbet off in the freezer for an hour or so, or until the mixture is hard enough to make a solid scoop.*

Zucchini Pudding Soufflés
with Creamy Tomato Sauce

I discovered twice-cooked pudding soufflés more than a decade ago, and they've been my favorite dinner party workhorse ever since. They have all the elegance and versatility of a "real" soufflé, without the stress of the last-minute prep. These can be prepared hours ahead of time, and I've made them with everything from chocolate to spinach, but this one all but screams summer when both zucchini and tomatoes are in ample supply.

Toss the grated zucchini and 1¾ teaspoons of the salt in a large bowl, then let sit for 30 minutes.

Butter six 4-ounce ramekins and dust with 2 tablespoons of the Parmesan.

Drain the zucchini, rinse well, and squeeze out excess water in handfuls, using paper towels.

Preheat the oven to 350°F.

Melt 2 tablespoons of the butter in a sauté pan over medium heat. Add the zucchini and sauté, tossing often and spreading out with a wooden spoon, until dried and lightly colored, 7 to 8 minutes. Set aside.

In a saucepan, melt the remaining 4 tablespoons butter over low heat. Add the flour, 1 tablespoon at a time, whisking to prevent lumps. Continue whisking for about 3 minutes, then add the milk and whisk until the sauce comes to a boil. Remove the pan from the heat and stir in the Gruyère and 1 tablespoon of the Parmesan. Let cool for about 2 minutes, then whisk in the egg yolks, one at a time. Stir in the zucchini, the remaining ¼ teaspoon salt, and a couple grindings of pepper.

In the bowl of a stand mixer fitted with a whisk attachment, beat the egg whites until stiff. Gently fold the egg whites into the zucchini mixture.

Spoon the mixture into the prepared ramekins until just more than three-quarters full. Sprinkle 1 tablespoon of the remaining Parmesan on top and set them into a deep baking dish (I use a Pyrex casserole dish). Pour enough hot water into the dish to reach halfway up the sides of the ramekins. Place on the middle rack of the oven and bake for about 25 minutes, until the puddings are puffed and lightly brown on top. Remove from the water bath and let cool for 10 minutes.

Makes 6 soufflés

1 pound zucchini, washed, trimmed, and coarsely grated

2 teaspoons salt

6 tablespoons unsalted butter, plus more for the ramekins

5 tablespoons finely grated Parmesan cheese

3 tablespoons all-purpose flour

1 cup whole milk

⅔ cup grated Gruyère cheese

3 large eggs, separated

Freshly ground black pepper

Creamy Tomato Sauce (recipe follows)

Run a knife around the inside edge of each ramekin and invert the soufflés into the palm of your hand or onto a small plate. Arrange the soufflés, browned-sides up and 1 inch apart, in a Pyrex or ceramic baking dish. (At this point, the soufflés can be held for several hours at room temperature.)

When ready to serve, increase the oven temperature to 400°F and prepare the tomato cream sauce. Pour the sauce over and around the puddings and sprinkle with the remaining 1 tablespoon Parmesan. Bake until the soufflés are puffed up again and the sauce is bubbling, 8 to 10 minutes. Serve each soufflé on a plate napped with a few teaspoons of the creamy tomato sauce.

Makes 3 cups

1 cup tomato puree
2 cups heavy cream
Salt and freshly ground black pepper
Cayenne pepper

Creamy Tomato Sauce

Whisk together the tomato puree and cream in a bowl. Season with salt, black pepper, and cayenne.

Tomato Tarte Tatin

've always loved tarte tatin, the French upside-down tart in which the fruit, usually apples or pears, is perfectly caramelized in butter and sugar. For years, the pear tarte tatin in *The Chez Panisse Menu Cookbook* was my go-to fall and winter dessert. But in summer, ripe tomatoes almost beg for the same treatment. The fennel seeds combined with the raw sugar are key here, and there's just enough sugar to bring out the tomatoes' natural sweetness. Still, this tarte tatin is a decidedly savory offering and would make an excellent main course alongside a green salad.

Preheat the oven to 275°F. Brush a 9-inch round baking pan with olive oil and line the bottom with a circle of parchment paper.

Toss the cherry tomatoes with 1 tablespoon of the olive oil, the garlic, a healthy pinch of salt, and a couple grindings of pepper. Place the tomatoes on a baking sheet and roast for 40 minutes.

Meanwhile, heat the remaining 2 tablespoons oil in a sauté pan or skillet over medium-low heat. Add the onion and a pinch of salt and cook, stirring occasionally, until golden brown, about 10 minutes. Remove from the heat.

When the tomatoes are done, remove them from the oven and increase the oven temperature to 400°F.

In a small skillet stir the fennel seeds with a wooden spoon over medium heat, for a minute or so, until they're "toasted" and you can smell their aroma, being careful not to let them burn. Add the butter to the skillet. Once it has melted, stir in the sugar and vinegar. Remove the fennel mixture from the heat and spread it over the bottom of the prepared baking pan. Scatter in the thyme and oregano leaves, then add the tomato slices in a single closely packed layer. Season with salt and pepper. Add the roasted cherry tomatoes, pressing to fill in any gaps. Add the sautéed onion and top evenly with the goat cheese.

Cut a round of puff pastry 1 inch larger than the diameter of the pan. Lay the pastry round over the tart filling and tuck the edges into the pan. Bake for 30 minutes. Lower the oven temperature to 350°F and bake for another 20 minutes, or until the pastry is completely cooked through.

Cool for 10 minutes and place a serving plate on the top of the pan. Hold the plate and pan firmly together and invert. Carefully lift off the pan and rearrange any tomatoes that may have become dislodged. Scatter the surface with more herb leaves, if you like.

Serves 4 as a main course, or 6 as a side dish or appetizer

3 tablespoons extra-virgin olive oil, plus more for oiling the baking pan

2 cups cherry tomatoes, halved

2 garlic cloves, finely chopped

Kosher salt and freshly ground black pepper

1 large onion, thinly sliced

2 teaspoons fennel seeds

2 tablespoons unsalted butter

2 tablespoons raw sugar

1½ teaspoons balsamic vinegar

Leaves from **3** thyme sprigs, plus more for garnish (optional)

Leaves from **1** oregano sprig, plus more for garnish (optional)

3 large heirloom tomatoes, cut into ¼-inch slices

8 ounces crumbled goat cheese (2 cups)

1 sheet frozen puff pastry, thawed

Sliced Chicken Breast
with Tomato Vinaigrette

Serves 6

FOR THE CHICKEN SLICES

One 3-pound chicken
Salt and freshly ground
    black pepper

FOR THE TOMATO VINAIGRETTE

¾ cup extra-virgin olive oil
1 tablespoon plus
    1 teaspoon fresh lemon
    juice
¾ teaspoon salt
¾ teaspoon sugar
½ teaspoon freshly ground
    black pepper
¾ cup tomato puree

Basil leaves or tarragon
    leaves for garnish

At one point during my college years, I was so broke that I took a part-time job selling cookbooks over the phone for Time Life. It turned out to be one of the best things that ever happened to me. The books were the now fabled *The Good Cook* series supervised by the great Richard Olney, with Jeremiah Tower acting as a consultant on some of the volumes. I think I lasted a month on the job, but I got a hell of a culinary education and I still refer to the books (some of which I won for being so passionate in the selling of them) all the time. In *Salads,* there's a step-by-step photographic essay explaining how to prepare this chicken recipe. I first made it more than thirty years ago and have never tired of its bright appearance and flavor.

TO MAKE THE CHICKEN SLICES

Preheat the oven to 325° F.

Season the bird's cavity with salt and pepper. Place the chicken in a shallow roasting pan, breast-side up, and roast for 1 hour. Remove the pan from the oven and let the chicken rest for 15 minutes.

Transfer the chicken to a large cutting board, steady the chicken with one hand, and, using a sharp knife, cut the skin between the thigh and the body. Bend the leg down to locate the hip joint and cut through it to sever the leg neatly. Now cut through the corner of the breast to the shoulder joint, then sever the wing from the body at the joint. Turn the bird over and remove the other leg and wing.

Return the legs to the oven for another 15 minutes, or until their juices run clear when the meat is pierced. Reserve the legs and wings for another use (or to have as a tasty snack).

Using the same sharp knife, start from the chicken's tail end and cut just below both sides of the rib cage to sever the breast from the backbone. When the breast is free, steady the bird with one hand. With your other hand, take hold of the edge of the skin at the narrow, pointed end of the breast and pull it away in one piece. To carve, steady one side of the breast with your fingertips and carve the opposite side into thin slices. Hold the breastbone while carving the second side of the breast.

TO MAKE THE TOMATO VINAIGRETTE

Place the olive oil, lemon juice, salt, sugar, pepper, and tomato puree in a blender. Blend until the mixture is smooth and the color is a rich red, about 1 minute. Taste for seasoning.

TO ASSEMBLE THE DISH

Spread the vinaigrette on a serving platter and arrange the slices of chicken breast in a pinwheel pattern on top. Garnish with a rosette of basil.

NOTE: *You can make the chicken and the vinaigrette and refrigerate them separately for up to 1 day ahead of time, but don't slice the breast until ready to serve lest it dry out. The chicken is meant to be served cold, but I like to bring both it and the sauce toward room temperature for 10 to 15 minutes.*

Almond Buttermilk Shortcakes
with Peaches Poached in Red Wine & White Chocolate Whipped Cream

When peaches are in season, I eat at least as many of them as I do tomatoes, usually leaning over the sink with the juice running down my chin. Because peaches and tomatoes go so well together, I often add peeled peaches to an heirloom tomato salad or chop equal amounts for a salsa with onion, mint, and jalapeño. Here, peaches do more traditional duty on their own as a filling for individual almond-flavored shortcakes. I poached the peaches for this recipe with a Zinfandel from Elyse Winery and we ate the finished shortcakes with a 2003 Zin from Ridge that I found in the back of a cupboard. The wine's velvety, mature tannins and notes of vanilla and clove, chocolate and berry (almost like a port) were nothing short of amazing with the dessert. If you can get your hands on a bottle, I'd highly recommend it!

TO MAKE THE SHORTCAKES

Preheat the oven to 425°F. Line a baking sheet with parchment paper.

Combine the flour, sugar, baking powder, baking soda, and salt in a large bowl and, using a pastry blender, two forks, or your fingers, cut in the pieces of butter until the mixture looks like coarse cornmeal. (You can also use a food processor for this, but I swear a pastry blender, the forks, or your fingers are just as easy.)

In a small bowl, combine the buttermilk, egg, and almond extract. Make a well in the center of the flour mixture and pour in the buttermilk mixture. Mix lightly, adding more buttermilk, if needed, to form a slightly sticky dough. Do not overmix.

Place the dough on a lightly floured surface and sprinkle more flour on the dough. Gently pat the dough to an even 1-inch thickness. Using a 3-inch round cookie cutter, cut out shortcakes and transfer to the baking sheet. Gather together the dough scraps to make the remaining shortcakes. Brush the milk over the shortcakes, scatter the almonds over the tops, and sprinkle lightly with the remaining 1 tablespoon sugar. Bake the shortcakes for 10 to 15 minutes, until golden. Cool slightly before serving.

Serves 6

FOR THE SHORTCAKES

2¼ cups all-purpose flour, plus more for kneading

⅓ cup sugar, plus 1 tablespoon for sprinkling over the shortcakes

1½ teaspoons baking powder

¼ teaspoon baking soda

¼ teaspoon salt

8 tablespoons (1 stick) cold unsalted butter, cut into small pieces

⅔ cup buttermilk

1 large beaten egg

1 teaspoon pure almond extract

1 tablespoon whole milk or cream

¼ cup sliced blanched almonds

FOR THE PEACHES

1½ cups water

1½ cups sugar

3 cups Zinfandel or other fruity, full-bodied red wine

3 pounds peaches, peeled, pitted, and cut into ¾-inch slices

FOR THE WHITE CHOCOLATE WHIPPED CREAM

8 ounces white chocolate, roughly chopped

1⅔ cups heavy cream

Mint leaves or Thai basil leaves for garnish

TO PREPARE THE PEACHES

Place the water, sugar, and wine in a large heavy saucepan and bring to a boil over high heat. Reduce the heat and simmer for 5 minutes. Add the peach slices and simmer for 10 minutes more.

Remove the pan from the heat and let the peaches come to room temperature in the syrup.

NOTE: *The poached peaches may be covered and refrigerated in the syrup for up to 2 days.*

TO MAKE THE WHITE CHOCOLATE WHIPPED CREAM

Combine the white chocolate and ⅔ cup of the cream in a small heavy saucepan over low heat, and cook stirring continuosly until the chocolate has melted. Remove the pan from the heat and transfer the mixture to a large bowl. Let stand for 15 to 20 minutes, until the mixture has cooled down a bit and started to thicken.

In the bowl of a stand mixer fitted with a whisk attachment, beat the remaining 1 cup cream until soft peaks form. Using a spatula, fold the whipped cream into the chocolate mixture in two batches. Cover and refrigerate for up to 1 day if not using immediately.

TO ASSEMBLE THE DESSERT

Using a serrated knife, split the shortcakes. Set the bottoms on dessert plates and spread with a bit of the white chocolate whipped cream. Crown with the lids, and serve more whipped cream on the side, along with the peaches poached in red wine. Garnish with mint or Thai basil leaves.

NOTE: *The addition of the white chocolate to the whipped cream means that it's almost like a mousse and, therefore, pretty substantial. In a pinch, you could skip the shortcakes and serve the cream in dessert cups, topping the poached peach slices, or vice versa.*

A MISSISSIPPI SANDBAR PICNIC

My hometown of Greenville, Mississippi, is—at least sort of—located on the river. A while ago the river changed course, and now we're technically on an oxbow lake called Lake Ferguson, but if you get in a boat at the foot of Main Street, the Mississippi is only about six miles away. Pretty much everyone I know grew up on a raft or in a speedboat or both, and a few years back, when the river was especially low, a group of us decided to drop anchor on an enormous sandbar my good friend Hank Burdine had found just under the bridge that connects Mississippi to Arkansas. We had a bucket of chicken, a cooler full of beer, and a couple of guitar players along for the ride. It turned out to be such a good idea we decided to institutionalize it.

Now we go out at least a few times a year, but we've significantly stepped up our game (and our style). We bring tables and lounge chairs, worn-out Oriental rugs, and lots of Indian quilts to spread on the sand. There's a ladies' room in the form of a tepee made from willows cut on the opposite bank, a full bar, and a grill set over a hole in the sand containing lit charcoal and driftwood. Paper plates and plastic cups have given way to enamel plates and cups and stemmed Lucite wineglasses. Tunes are provided by the official Sandbar Boom Box, a masterpiece of Burdine engineering consisting of an ice chest with holes cut into one side for speakers and a car CD player installed on the inside and rigged with twenty feet of wire attached with alligator clips to a 12-volt battery. Our captains are Hank (a commissioner of the Mississippi Levee Board), Bo Weevil (aka Sid Law, who's run the entire length of the Mississippi in his custom flat-bottom boat), and Howard Brent (who once owned one of the biggest towboat companies on the river). They get us out there early and we stay late, returning—if we're lucky—beneath a glorious buttermilk sky (covered in so many altocumulus clouds it looks like clabbered buttermilk) just as the sun is setting.

Now that we have real plates and even "silverware" {bamboo-handled forks and spoons from William-Wayne & Co. (see Sources, page 219)}, our menu is far more ambitious than our initial drive-through fare from the Colonel. We start off with marinated shrimp and the delicious catfish-and-caper mousse available from Taste of Gourmet in Indianola, Mississippi (see Sources, page 219). We heat up barbecue on our makeshift grill, fill bowls with corn and potato salads, and sometimes I get ambitious and make the homemade dill batter loaf from my old *Joy of Cooking*, but any good yeasty loaf will do. I highly recommend dining (and dancing and singing) under the sun in the middle of the mighty Mississippi. But this menu would work just as well under a tree or on a porch—anywhere there are good friends and fun.

SANDBAR PLAYLIST

• Come on Down to My Boat
Every Mother's Son

• Mississippi Queen
Mountain

• The Captain
Kasey Chambers

• Proud Mary
Ike & Tina Turner

• Ol' Man River
Jeff Beck

• Barefootin'
Wilson Pickett

• Watching the River Flow
Bob Dylan

• Sailin' Shoes/ Hey Julia
Robert Palmer

• Ole Buttermilk Sky
Willie Nelson

• Lipstick Sunset
John Hiatt

The Menu

THE EVENING STORM

MARINATED SHRIMP
*with Catfish Mousse
and Baked Saltines*

BARBECUED
PORK SHOULDER

DECONSTRUCTED
STREET CORN

NEW POTATOES
with Garlic and Mint

CHESS PIE SQUARES

THE EVENING STORM

I think Suzanne Goin is one of the best chefs in the country, and whenever I'm in Los Angeles, I eat lunch at A.O.C. and dinner at Lucques. The charming Christiaan Rollich, a mix master of uncommon skill, creates cocktails for both restaurants. I had the good fortune of meeting Christiaan behind the bar at A.O.C. one day, and before I'd finished lunch, I'd convinced him to come up with a cocktail for this book. On my way to L.A., I'd stopped off to see a retrospective of paintings and sculpture by my friend the über-talented David Bates, at the Modern Art Museum of Fort Worth. While there, I had lunch with David and his lovely wife, Jan, at the museum's café, and David, an avid fisherman, ordered up a drink made with his favorite Flor de Caña seven-year-old rum. The show featured a painting I've long loved called *Evening Storm*, so the inspiration for the drink was born. I sent an image of the work to Christiaan, and he sent this recipe back. Thank goodness we've never actually encountered a storm during any of our sandbar escapades, but Christiaan's cocktail certainly leads to some high spirits. I hope only that he and David and Jan can join us on the river someday soon.

3 cups Flor de Caña Grand Reserve

1 cup Calvados

1½ cups Velvet Falernum liqueur

1½ cups fresh lemon juice

1 cup brewed black tea

1 cup pineapple juice

2 cups Champagne

1 cup fresh pineapple slices or chunks

¾ cup blackberries

1 orange, sliced

1 lemon, sliced

Combine the Flor de Caña, Calvados, Velvet Falernum, lemon juice, tea, and pineapple juice in a large pitcher and stir well. Add the Champagne (a good sparkling wine like Roederer Estate Brut would also be fine) and stir in the pineapple, blackberries, orange, and lemon. Chill and serve on the rocks in whatever picnic cup you have handy.

Marinated Shrimp

Serves 6 to 8 as hors d'oeuvres

2 pounds (16 to 20 count) shrimp, shelled, shells reserved

6 garlic cloves

1 teaspoon kosher salt, plus more to taste

2 teaspoons whole black peppercorns

1 tablespoon fresh lime juice, plus more for finishing

¼ cup extra-virgin olive oil

2 bay leaves

Baked Saltines (recipe follows) for serving

Most Southerners I know have a thing for pickled shrimp, but I've never been a fan. The vinegar and pickling spices invariably overpower the shrimp's sweet taste, and the texture is inevitably a tad mushy. I based this far less strident recipe on one for peppered oysters from the great Diana Kennedy, the Julia Child of Mexican cuisine. You can serve it with toasted baguette slices or pretty much any cracker, but I love it with the buttery baked saltines below. The sprinkling of Old Bay Seasoning on the cracker is a subtle nod to the seasoning in a classic pickled shrimp.

Using the shells from the shrimp, make the shrimp stock according to the directions on page 22. Reduce it down to a fairly intense concentration and set aside 4 tablespoons, reserving the rest for another use.

Trim the root end from each garlic clove and press the flat side of a chef's knife down on each clove to loosen the peel. Remove the peels and sprinkle the cloves with ½ teaspoon of the salt. Finely mince the garlic and press down again with the flat side of the knife to make a rough paste with the salt. Scrape the paste into a small bowl.

Coarsely grind the peppercorns. (If you don't have a grinder that can coarsely grind the pepper, lay the peppercorns on a dish towel and smash them with a rolling pin.) Add the remaining ½ teaspoon salt and the coarsely ground peppercorns. Gradually add the lime juice and mix well. Stir in 3 tablespoons of the shrimp stock.

Heat the olive oil in a large skillet over medium-high heat. Add the bay leaves and the garlic mixture and cook for about 2 minutes, shaking the pan and stirring often. Add the shrimp and cook for 2 to 3 minutes more, still shaking the pan and stirring to make sure the shrimp are pink on both sides.

Remove the skillet from the heat. Taste the shrimp to make sure they are just cooked through and add more salt if necessary. Finish by stirring in a squeeze of lime juice and the remaining 1 tablespoon shrimp stock. If the shrimp need a bit more cooking, return them to the fire for another minute or two, but do not overcook the shrimp.

Serve immediately or at room temperature. When the shrimp have cooled, you may cover and refrigerate them, but remove the shrimp 20 to 30 minutes before serving. Accompany them with the baked saltines.

Baked Saltines

Makes about 40 crackers

1 sleeve Nabisco Premium Saltine crackers

4 tablespoons (½ stick) butter, melted

Old Bay Seasoning for sprinkling

Preheat oven to 350°F.

Place the saltine crackers in a single layer on a baking sheet. Use a pastry brush to baste the saltines with a layer of the butter and sprinkle each cracker with Old Bay. Bake for 5 to 7 minutes, until golden. Let cool, and store in an airtight container until ready to serve.

Barbecued Pork Shoulder

This recipe is from one of my favorite cookbooks in the world, *Lee Bailey's Country Weekends*, and I've been making it—a lot—since the book came out in 1983. The late, great Lee used a veal shoulder, but because veal shoulders are increasingly hard to find, I've substituted pork. I've also prepared the recipe with a butterflied veal loin for a "fancy" barbecue supper. But I honestly think Bailey's vegetable marinade would enhance almost anything.

Using a heavy sharp knife, cut a deep pocket into one side of the pork roast, cutting almost all the way through to the other side, so that you can lay the meat out almost flat. Rub with salt and black pepper and place in a deep baking dish. Set aside.

Place the scallions, onion, bell pepper, parsley, and garlic in the bowl of a food processor and pulse until the mixture is cut to medium bits.

Heat the peanut oil in a large skillet over medium heat and add the contents of the food processor. Simmer for 5 minutes and stir in the tomato sauce, vinegar, Worcestershire sauce, honey, capers, and Tabasco. Simmer for another 20 minutes. Taste for seasonings and cool.

Pour the marinade over the meat, making sure the meat is completely covered. Cover and refrigerate for at least 5 hours or overnight, turning the meat once or twice.

About 1 hour before cooking, remove the meat from the refrigerator. Prepare coals for a barbecue or heat a gas grill, and preheat the oven to 375°F. When the grill is ready, remove the meat from the marinade (making sure to reserve the marinade), and grill each side for 15 minutes.

Meanwhile, heat the reserved marinade in a saucepan. Place the meat back in the deep casserole, pour the heated sauce around it, and cover. Bake in the oven for 1 hour. If the meat is still tough, bake for up to 30 minutes longer.

When ready to serve, slice the meat and spoon some sauce over each portion. Serve any leftover sauce on the side.

One 5- to 6-pound boneless pork shoulder

1 teaspoon kosher salt, plus more for seasoning

Freshly ground black pepper

2 bunches scallions, trimmed and cut in half, some green tops included

1 large yellow onion, cut into chunks

1 green bell pepper, seeded, stemmed, and cut into chunks

8 Italian parsley sprigs, roughly chopped

3 large garlic cloves

½ cup peanut oil

½ cup canned tomato sauce

½ cup red wine vinegar or sherry vinegar

¼ cup Lea & Perrins Worcestershire sauce

¼ cup honey

1 tablespoon drained capers

¼ teaspoon Tabasco sauce

Deconstructed Street Corn

Serves 6 to 8

Mexican "street corn"—grilled corn on the cob slathered with some combination of mayonnaise, lime juice, chili powder, and crumbly cotija cheese—is so wildly popular north of the border that Mario Batali has even done an Italian version, substituting balsamic vinegar for the lime juice and Parmesan for the cotija. Both are super tasty (if seriously messy), but hardly picnic fare. The same ingredients can be added to a quick sauté of corn shaved off the cob. I use Batali's Mediterranean ingredients here, but a version using the Mexican ingredients (plus some fresh cilantro) would also be swell.

Heat the olive oil in a large skillet over low heat. Add the jalapeño and sauté for 2 minutes. Increase the heat to medium, add the corn and salt, and cook, stirring occasionally, for 5 minutes.

In a large bowl, toss the corn mixture, mint, and vinegar. Add the Parmesan and toss again. Serve cold or at room temperature.

2 tablespoons olive oil

1 jalapeño pepper, stemmed, seeded, and finely chopped

6 cups fresh corn kernels (shaved from about **12** ears)

Pinch of salt

¼ cup chopped mint or basil leaves, or a mixture of both

2 tablespoons balsamic vinegar

⅓ cup grated Parmesan cheese

New Potatoes with Garlic and Mint

Serves 6 to 8

I don't think I've ever been to a warm-weather party hosted by Mary Thomas Joseph, my lifelong friend and frequent cooking partner, when she hasn't served this dish. It's delicious, easily toteable, and far more durable in the heat than a mayonnaise-based potato salad.

Place the potatoes in a large pot with enough water to cover by about 2 inches. Add 2 teaspoons of the salt and bring to a boil over high heat. Reduce the heat and boil gently until the potatoes are tender when pierced with the tip of a knife, 15 to 18 minutes. Drain.

As soon as the potatoes are cool enough to handle, cut them into quarters or halves, depending on their size. Place them in a large mixing or serving bowl, and immediately toss with the olive oil, the remaining 1 teaspoon salt, and the pepper. Gently toss in the garlic and mint, making sure the potatoes are coated with both. Let sit for a few minutes to absorb the flavors. Taste for seasonings. Serve warm or at room temperature. The dish may be covered and refrigerated, but remove 45 minutes before serving.

3 pounds new potatoes, scrubbed, with skin on

3 teaspoons kosher salt

½ cup extra-virgin olive oil

½ teaspoon freshly ground black pepper

8 garlic cloves, minced

½ cup chopped mint leaves

Chess Pie Squares

I love chess pie and I love lemon squares, and this recipe is a sort of combo of the two. No one wants to slice pie at a picnic, and I serve lemon squares so much that I wanted a change of pace for this occasion. These, developed with the amazingly talented New Orleans–based pastry chef Beth Biundo (see Sources, page 219), turned out to be a big hit and are now permanent fixtures in my arsenal of pick-up desserts.

Preheat the oven to 350°F.

TO MAKE THE SHORTBREAD CRUST

Sift the flour, sugar, and salt into a large bowl. Cut in the butter with a pastry blender or two forks until well blended and the dough holds together when you press a lump in your hand.

Press the dough evenly into the bottom of 9 by 13-inch baking dish. Bake until the edges begin to brown, about 15 minutes. Remove the shortbread from the oven and allow to cool slightly. Reduce the oven temperature to 325°F.

TO MAKE THE FILLING

In the bowl of a stand mixer fitted with the whisk attachment, cream the butter and sugar. Beat in the egg yolks until well blended, then beat in the buttermilk and vanilla. Beat in the cornmeal and flour.

Pour the filling over the crust. Bake for 25 minutes, or until the top is golden and set. Cool in the dish on a wire rack and cut the dessert into 24 squares to serve.

Makes about 24 squares

FOR THE SHORTBREAD CRUST

2 cups all-purpose flour

½ cup confectioners' sugar

½ teaspoon salt

6 ounces (1½ sticks) butter, softened

FOR THE FILLING

6 ounces (1½ sticks) butter

1½ cups sugar

6 large egg yolks

2 teaspoons pure vanilla extract

¾ cup buttermilk

2 tablespoons white cornmeal

2 tablespoons all-purpose flour

A FALL HUNT BREAKFAST

The opening day of dove season in the Delta is the unofficial beginning of fall and an occasion that inevitably calls for a post-hunt celebration. This particular kickoff was held at the Glen Allan, Mississippi, Highland Club, founded in 1893 as a place for the men in the area to gamble. Located on the banks of Lake Washington (one of the many oxbow lakes formed when the Mississippi changed its course), it's also down the road from the sunflower field where the hunters tried their luck just after sunrise that day.

When I was a kid, we'd catch crappie and bream in the lake, and the club cook would clean and fry them for us. These days we do lots of the cooking ourselves, and in planning this menu, I chose to avoid classic (but heavy) hunt breakfast fare like grillades and grits and hot fruit compote. Dove season may well herald fall, but September in Mississippi is not exactly chilly.

The smoked trout hash at the menu's center is substantial enough for hungry hunters but still relatively light, with flavors that are sharp and bright (and colors to match). I compromised with one hot-and-cheesy thing, the mushroom bread pudding, but the fruit is fresh rather than baked. To start, you could offer anything from a ham biscuit to a cinnamon roll from the trusty Sister Schubert's (see Sources, page 219).

The serving pieces, plates, and even the drinking cups are all part of my collection of McCartys Pottery, founded in 1954 in a barn in nearby Merigold, Mississippi, by Lee and Pup McCarty. Made of Mississippi mud, each piece bears the trademarked black squiggly line that signifies the river, and many now reside in museum collections across the country. Lee and Pup were dear friends and great characters, and a trip to the studio (and exquisite gardens) remains a treat. Pup died in 2009, and Lee left us in his sleep, at ninety-two, as this manuscript was being completed. I will miss Lee's enormous generosity of spirit, but his work continues in the capable hands of his godson Jamie Smith, who worked side by side with him for decades.

When I first saw the fabric used for the tablecloths here—yet another gorgeous pattern by Peter Fasano—I thought it must have been designed to match the McCarty colors. At that point, Peter and his wife, the equally talented designer Elizabeth Hamilton, had not, in fact, been introduced to the pottery. Since then, they've made the trek to Merigold twice and started their own burgeoning collection, a pursuit I highly recommend.

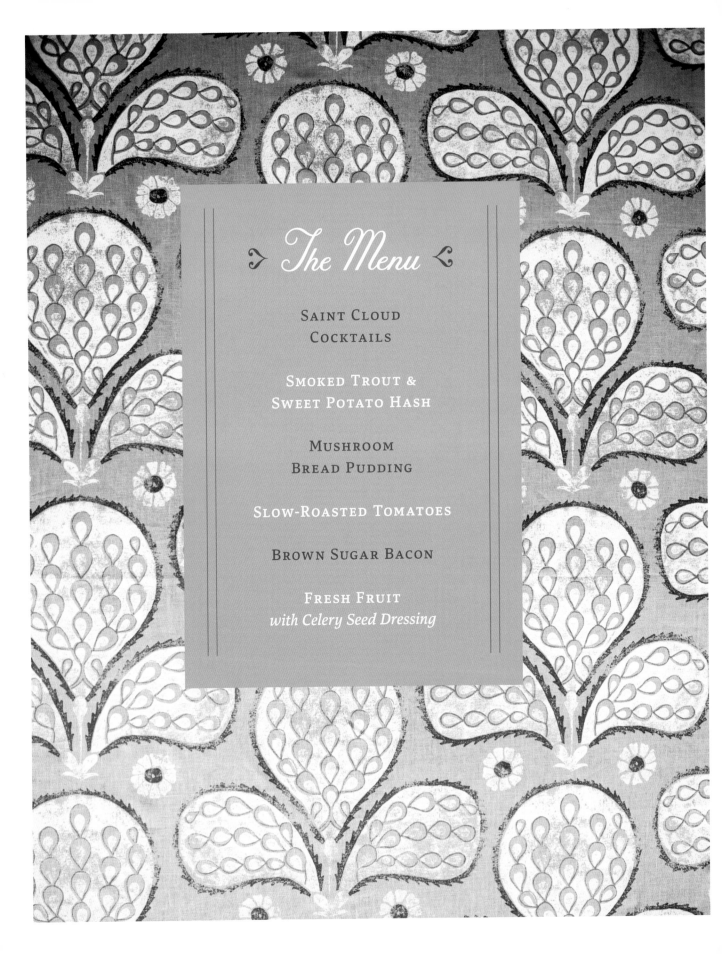

The Menu

Saint Cloud
Cocktails

Smoked Trout &
Sweet Potato Hash

Mushroom
Bread Pudding

Slow-Roasted Tomatoes

Brown Sugar Bacon

Fresh Fruit
with Celery Seed Dressing

The Saint Cloud

My lifelong friends and Delta neighbors the noted caterers and party givers Carl and Amanda Cottingham discovered this delicious grapefruit juice–based cocktail at Aquitaine, a restaurant in Boston's South End. When Carl approximated the Saint Cloud in his Greenville kitchen, I vowed to go straight to the source on my next trip north. At the restaurant, the drink is made in a shaker and served straight up with a dusting of lime zest on top. But it also makes a great pitcher drink. The rosemary simple syrup is genius with the grapefruit juice, which has an especially pretty color when squeezed from Ruby Reds.

Combine the water and sugar in a medium saucepan. Bring to a boil over high heat and cook until the sugar has just dissolved.

Remove from the heat and steep the rosemary sprigs in the syrup. Allow the mixture to cool for 30 minutes to 1 hour. Remove the rosemary and strain the syrup into a container with a lid. Refrigerate the rosemary syrup until ready to use. I keep it in a mason jar for up to 1 month.

When ready to make the drink, combine the grapefruit juice and vodka in a tall pitcher. Add the rosemary syrup to taste. For a mixture this large, I usually end up adding 1 cup, but you should start with ¾ cup and taste. Stir in the lime zest, if using, and pour into highball or collins glasses filled with ice. Garnish with a rosemary sprig.

Serves 8

2 cups water

2 cups sugar

1 bunch rosemary sprigs, plus more for garnish

6 cups fresh grapefruit juice, strained and chilled

4 cups vodka, well chilled

1 tablespoon lime zest (optional)

Smoked Trout
and Sweet Potato Hash

Serves 6 to 8

Feel free to play around with the herbs in this recipe. You could add parsley and/or dill or replace the tarragon with thyme leaves.

Melt 2 tablespoons of the butter with 1 tablespoon of the olive oil in a large skillet or sauté pan over medium-high heat. Add the onion and celery and sauté until translucent, about 5 minutes. Season with salt and pepper. Add the garlic and 1 tablespoon of the tarragon. Cook for another 30 seconds. Add the russet potatoes and season with more salt and pepper. Cook, stirring frequently, until the russet potatoes are tender, 15 to 20 minutes. Remove from the heat and set aside.

In a separate large skillet over medium-high heat, melt the remaining 2 tablespoons butter with the remaining 1 tablespoon oil and add the sweet potatoes. Season with salt and pepper and cook, stirring frequently, until tender, about 15 minutes.

Place the skillet with the russet potatoes over medium heat. Add the sweet potatoes and the remaining 1 tablespoon tarragon and toss together. Cook for 2 to 3 minutes. Add the chives and smoked trout, torn into large flakes. Cook for another minute or two, long enough to warm the trout. Serve with the sauce Maltaise on the side.

4 tablespoons (½ stick) butter

2 tablespoons olive oil

½ cup diced onion

½ cup chopped celery

Kosher salt and freshly ground black pepper

2 garlic cloves, minced

2 tablespoons tarragon leaves

1 pound russet potatoes, peeled and cut into ½-inch cubes

1 pound sweet potatoes, peeled and cut into ½-inch cubes

1 tablespoon minced chives

1 pound smoked trout fillets, skinned

Blender Sauce Maltaise

Makes 1½ cups

Sauce Maltaise is hollandaise flavored with orange juice and orange zest. This blender version based on a recipe from Julia Child is insanely easy, foolproof, and delicious—and great on asparagus!

Place the egg yolks, salt, a pinch of cayenne, the lemon juice, and orange juice in the jar of a blender. Blend for 2 seconds at top speed. With the blender still running, add hot, melted butter in a thin stream. Add the orange zest. Taste and add more juice, orange zest, or seasonings as needed. Depending on the sweetness of the oranges, you may need another tablespoon of juice.

6 large egg yolks

¼ teaspoon salt

Cayenne pepper

2 tablespoons each fresh lemon and orange juices

½ pound (2 sticks) butter

Grated zest of **2 oranges**

Mushroom Bread Pudding

Serves 6 to 8

1 tablespoon butter, plus more for greasing the baking dish

1 medium yellow onion, chopped

½ teaspoon dried marjoram

1 teaspoon dried thyme

¼ cup dry white wine

1 tablespoon olive oil

1 pound button or baby bella mushrooms, sliced irregularly

½ teaspoon kosher salt, plus more for seasoning

Freshly ground black pepper

3 large eggs

2 cups whole milk

¼ cup chopped scallions, including some of the tender green parts

8 slices firm white bread, such as Pepperidge Farm

2 cups mixed grated cheeses, such as Parmesan, Gruyère, and smoked Gouda

ike Alice Waters's *The Chez Panisse Menu Cookbook*, Deborah Madison's *The Greens Cookbook* heralded—and nurtured—a sea change in American cuisine when it was published in 1987. I'm pretty sure I've cooked everything in it at least once. This pudding, adapted from a recipe in the book, is one of my go-to brunch dishes. It's also great for using up odds and ends of cheeses in your fridge. I am especially fond of the combination of smoked Gouda and Parmesan.

Preheat the oven to 375°F. Butter a 9 by 13-inch baking dish or a deep-dish pie plate.

Melt the butter in a large skillet over medium heat and add the onion. Crumble the marjoram and thyme between your fingers onto the onion and cook until the onion is soft, 10 to 15 minutes, stirring occasionally. When the mixture begins to get dry, add the white wine.

Add the olive oil to the onion mixture, raise the heat to medium-high, and add the mushrooms. Stir until the mushrooms are coated with oil, season with salt and pepper, and cook for 3 to 4 minutes more, stirring frequently. Remove the skillet from the heat and set aside.

In a medium bowl, beat the eggs. Whisk in the milk. Stir in the salt and scallions and set aside.

Trim the crusts from the bread and slice the pieces in half. Arrange half of the slices over the bottom of the prepared dish, trimming the bread to fill in the empty spaces. Spoon the mushroom mixture and then half the grated cheese over the bread. Top the cheese with the remaining bread and cheese.

Pour the egg mixture over the top and cover with aluminum foil. Bake for 20 minutes. Remove the foil and continue baking for another 15 minutes, until the pudding is set.

Slow-Roasted Tomatoes

Broiled tomatoes are one of my absolute pet peeves. They don't stay in the oven long enough for the tomato flavor to deepen, and the texture is sort of a mess. These little gems, on the other hand, are super tomatoey and add a gorgeous spot of color to almost any menu.

Preheat the oven to 250°F.

Slice the tomatoes in half lengthwise and scoop out the seeds. Place the tomatoes upright in a 9 by 13-inch ovenproof dish. Sprinkle with salt and pepper. Place a dab of the pressed garlic and a thyme sprig in the center of each half. Drizzle generously with olive oil.

Bake for 2½ hours and serve warm or at room temperature.

Serves 8

12 ripe plum tomatoes
Kosher salt and freshly ground black pepper
4 garlic cloves, pressed
4 or 5 thyme sprigs
Extra-virgin olive oil

Brown Sugar Bacon

This addictive bacon is best—and crispiest—when made with a regular, thin-sliced variety. Sometimes I cut the pieces in half (after baking, before the final 5 minutes of cooling) and serve them as hors d'oeuvres with drinks.

Preheat the oven to 400°F. Line a large rimmed baking sheet with aluminum foil and set a rack over the foil.

Combine the sugar, black pepper, dry mustard, and a healthy pinch of cayenne in a large bowl. Toss the bacon in the mixture, making sure it is completely coated.

Arrange the bacon in a single layer on the rack over the baking sheet. Bake, rotating the pan halfway through, until the sugar has melted and the bacon is brown and shiny, 30 to 40 minutes. Cool on the rack for about 5 minutes, then loosen the slices from the rack with a metal spatula and place on a serving platter. Continue to cool for another 5 minutes before serving. The bacon will crisp more as it cools.

Serves 6 to 8

1½ cups packed dark brown sugar
2 teaspoons freshly ground black pepper
1 teaspoon dry mustard
Cayenne pepper
1 pound sliced bacon

Fresh Fruit
with Celery Seed Dressing

Serves 8

1 ripe cantaloupe, cut into 1½-inch chunks

1 pineapple, cut into 1½-inch chunks

1 bunch green seedless grapes

1 bunch red seedless grapes

2 cups strawberries, trimmed and halved

Celery Seed Dressing

Makes about 2 cups

½ cup sugar

1 teaspoon celery seeds

1 teaspoon salt

1 teaspoon dry mustard

1 teaspoon paprika

¼ cup apple cider vinegar

1 cup vegetable oil, or other neutral-flavored oil like canola

When I was a child, I don't think I ever saw a bowl of fresh fruit unaccompanied by celery seed dressing. It was (and still is) a mainstay on Greenville's Sunday country club buffet, as well as in my mother's kitchen. I copied this recipe from Mama's own handwritten files when I left for college, and I still love it. Plan on about a cup of fruit per person. Here, I used a mix of cantaloupe, red and green seedless grapes, strawberries, and pineapple, but anything goes. Honeydew and cantaloupe, for example, look especially pretty with blackberries. And for a more elegant presentation, I bother to use a melon baller.

Mix the cantaloupe, pineapple, green grapes, red grapes, and strawberries in a large serving bowl. Toss the fruit with the dressing, or serve it on the side.

Celery Seed Dressing

Combine the sugar, celery seeds, salt, dry mustard, and paprika in the bowl of a stand mixer fitted with the whisk attachment. Mix in the vinegar and slowly add the oil. Continue mixing until the dressing is thick and shiny.

THE VISITING DIGNITARY DINNER

I should say up front that V.D. does not stand for an embarrassing social disease, though among my family and friends it is indeed a social term. It stands, rather, for Visiting Dignitary. In the 1960s and '70s, when I was growing up, Mississippi was undergoing dramatic social and political change, and my father was smack in the middle of the action. Reporters loved to make the trek to see him, not least because they knew that he and his friend Hodding Carter III, our then newspaper editor, would take them for a steak at Greenville's legendary Doe's Eat Place or, better yet, bring them home to our house, where they were well entertained by my mother. One particular *New York Times* reporter got so comfortable so often that it was not uncommon for me to step over him in our living room on my way to the school bus. But the journalists, as much as my impressionable self thrilled to their presence, were not necessarily considered V.D.s—at least not until Bill Buckley was the visitor in question. On two days' notice, my father announced to my mother that Buckley and his wife, Pat, were coming to town, and wouldn't it be nice to have a dinner party?

It would have been fine except that our house had just been ripped apart in preparation for a remodel and there weren't door frames on most of the doors. No matter. It was decided that much of the evening would take place outside. Mama and her best friend, Bossy McGee, bought a ton of white wicker chairs and staple-gunned pale green cotton duck to the threadbare seat covers. A fireman who moonlighted as a painter came over at two in the morning to reattach and re-paint the door frames just in case. A menu, which Bossy dubbed the V.D. Dinner, was devised, and its contents have changed strikingly little since then. There is always either beef tenderloin or a rib-eye roast, scalloped oysters, and a casserole made of artichoke hearts, cream cheese, and spinach, now named, of course, V.D. spinach (and so good the reluctant writer Amanda Hesser had no choice but to include in *The Essential New York Times Cookbook*). In the early days, Uncle Ben's Long Grain & Wild Rice was served without embarrassment; baskets of homemade yeast rolls were always on the table. Dessert was and remains either charlotte russe or chocolate mousse, and for the inaugural event there were also petits fours with coffee.

Just before the party, I went with Daddy to meet his little plane, which had picked up the Buckleys in Memphis. Pat, whom I later came to adore, changed into what I knew, even then, to be a very chic Bill Blass sheath, and on the way to our house we passed a shopping center where a stretch limo was parked alongside a huge blinking sign that screamed "SEE JFK'S DEATH CAR!" She quite rightly pronounced it "barbaric" and likely had visions of some cross burners and the ghost of Governor Bilbo running around out there in the darkness. Thankfully, the subsequent swell time erased all that. Guests helped themselves from silver serving dishes in the dining room and sat on the newly "upholstered" chairs around tables on the terrace. After supper, Buckley took a seat at the piano. When I was finally forced to go to bed, everyone was singing along to a boisterous rendition of *Cielito Lindo,* and Bossy's niece was dancing on the table. Before Pat left, she asked my mother for the scalloped oyster recipe.

After such a triumph, the menu was pretty much set in stone, enabling it to be produced on a moment's notice—which was a good thing because the V.D.s kept arriving. Elliot Richardson turned up just before Richard Nixon sacked him as attorney general in the "Saturday Night Massacre." Ronald Reagan came a couple of years prior to launching his 1976 presidential run (and the bartender complimented him on "that movie where you didn't have any legs"). A lot of official Washington dined on beef and oysters baked with Ritz cracker crumbs in those years, but a V.D. menu is a useful thing to have up your sleeve even if you're not cooking for cabinet members. In *Julia Child's Menu Cookbook,* she includes a

"Dinner for the Boss," featuring, not surprisingly, beef tenderloin and chocolate mousse.

We all have our very own V.D.s and V.D. occasions: special birthdays of close friends and family, moments meant to be marked and shared. They demand a proper menu, but not one so dazzling or pretentious that it becomes a distraction, or worse, part of the conversation. Whether you're talking about matters of state or simply celebrating the accomplishments of someone you love, the food shouldn't be the point. It should, however, be delicious in that old-fashioned, sort of glamorous way my mother has always had a handle on.

Ronald Reagan came a couple of years prior to launching his 1976 presidential run

This menu is a prime example, which is why I think it has stood the test of time, though there has been the occasional tweak. When Mama serves it, she often adds a Bibb lettuce, grapefruit, and avocado salad in salad crescents placed alongside the plates. We both still offer yeast rolls (now supplied by Sister Schubert, see Sources, page 219), but we long ago forwent the Uncle Ben's—I go with a similarly dated (but very tasty) consommé rice pilaf and Mama usually replaces it with corn pudding. And while I remain loyal to V.D. spinach, I now opt for a slightly less rich and more elegant spinach puree, and I often include the slow-roasted tomatoes on page 137 for color.

⌁ The Menu ⌁

Rib-eye Roast

Mary's
Mustard Mousse

Horseradish Mousse

Scalloped Oysters

Jason's Spinach

Consommé Rice Pilaf

Charlotte
Russe

A NOTE ON THE OCCASION

V. D. also stands for "Very Dear"

The Visiting Dignitary honored at the dinner pictured here was my friend the playwright and screenwriter Robert Harling. The occasion was the twenty-fifth anniversary of his play *Steel Magnolias*, which, as the world knows, was subsequently made into a wildly successful and completely wonderful film. Bobby and I met when we were seated together at a dinner party, where we discussed prime rib and Jeremiah Tower's provocative suggestion that the best wine to serve it with is Château d'Yquem. By the end of the evening, we'd become fast friends, and within weeks I'd driven to his Natchitoches, Louisiana, plantation to test the great Mr. Tower's theory (it's a good one). Since then, we've traveled the world together, eating and generally having a fine time, but we also dine frequently at each other's tables. Mine, thanks to Bobby's endless generosity, is considerably well endowed. The man has given me so much stuff (ranging from silver sauce spoons and Laguiole knives to the marvelous old set of Blue Willow china we ate off at the Tomatopalooza on page 89) that I've come up with whole menus designed especially to show it all off. It was a great gift to be able to celebrate Bobby with this menu, because in his case, V.D. also stands for "Very Dear".

A NOTE ON THE TABLE SETTING

Twenty years ago, my mother announced that she wanted to start collecting smallish wine decanters so that guests at festive dinners such as this one could have their very own at each place setting. At the time, I was dating a series of Londoners, so on each trip over I'd hit the Portobello Road's Saturday market and scoop up one or two. Finds like those are few and far between at today's market, alas, though Riedel makes some of similar size. In the end, I amassed a dozen (thus fulfilling the maternal Christmas and birthday requirements for years on end) and they turned out to be a brilliant idea. Not only are they beautiful on the table, they add to the festivity by keeping the wine flowing

(though Mama hedges her bets with a larger backup decanter on the sideboard just behind her own seat).

The decanters are also handy for propping up place cards. The place cards featured here are from Erika Jack, the talented stationer from Charlottesville, Virginia (see Sources, page 219), who also wrote the event's reminders. (For relatively formal dinners like this, I invite people on the phone, followed by notes "To Remind.") I am crazy for Erika's colors, her papers, and her exuberant technique—no matter what she writes I see the word "celebrate" just beyond it.

The flowers are exuberant too, inspired by my favorite Herend Printemps dinner plates, which boast a different hand-painted bouquet in the center of each. There are six bouquets in all, and it's too much fun not to try to replicate at least some of them. I should add for observant readers that this dinner is the one time I break my no-after-dinner-coffee rule and use the Printemps demitasse cups for the purpose for which they were actually intended (rather than for the duck étouffée on pages 178 and 206). I put the dessert (and plates and spoons) on the sideboard along with an urn of coffee, tiny bites like sugared almonds and chocolate-covered orange rind, and good brandy (always Germain-Robin Select Barrel XO). Guests help themselves and return to the table or the nearby sofas to continue eating, drinking, talking, and, yes, even smoking.

Rib-eye Roast

There's no question that a standing rib roast is dramatic, but boy, is this boneless version easy to cook and to serve. The good news is that it's just as crunchy and crackly on the outside and as meltingly delicious on the inside. My mother has long been a proponent of the "closed door method," and I've eaten the results enough times to know I should use it too. You multiply the weight of the meat by 5 minutes, cook it exactly that long, turn the oven off, and walk away. It's that simple. It also results in a pretty perfect medium-rare roast. Mama is also a self-avowed lily gilder—hence the slathering of butter on an already fairly fatty piece of meat, but that (plus a heavy hand with the salt) is how you encourage that crackly business, which to me is pretty much the whole point. At home I still get chased out of the kitchen for cadging bits of the crust.

Three hours before you're ready to cook, remove the roast from the refrigerator and place in a shallow roasting pan. Sprinkle the meat all over with Worcestershire sauce and rub it in with your hands. Coat the meat all over with softened butter. Don't be stingy—the roast should look like a lightly iced cake. Sprinkle liberally with salt and pepper. Set aside, uncovered.

About 30 minutes before cooking, preheat the oven to 500°F.

Place the roast in the oven and bake for exactly 5 minutes per pound. (If your roast is exactly 8 pounds, cook it for exactly 40 minutes. This is what your calculator is for.) As soon as the baking time is complete, turn off the oven but do not open the oven door. Put up a sign—do whatever you have to do—but leave the meat inside for another 1½ hours.

Remove the roast to a carving board and slice. Because the meat has already "rested" in the oven, it doesn't need to rest further.

Serves 10

One 8- to 10-pound
  boneless rib roast
Lea & Perrins
  Worcestershire sauce
Butter, softened
Kosher salt and freshly
  ground black pepper

Mary's Mustard Mousse

Serves 16 as a condiment

Both the mustard and horseradish mousses on this menu are meant to be condiments of sorts for the beef. You could, of course, pass the horseradish sauce or the hot mustard featured in "A Christmas Cocktail Supper" on page 177. But the unmolded mousses look so pretty on the table, they add a far more interesting texture, and besides, no Southerner ever met an envelope of gelatin he or she didn't like. (In *Gourmet of the Delta*, a cookbook put together by a group of Episcopal churchwomen in Hollandale and Leland, Mississippi, there are seventy-seven salad recipes and fifty-eight of them call for either flavored Jell-O or unflavored gelatin.)

I was introduced to the mustard mousse by my friend Mary Sferruzza, a talented interior designer and seriously gifted cook. Such is her spot-on taste (her house in Greenville is one of my favorites anywhere) that in her hands even something as seemingly old school as a gelatin mold can seem remarkably sophisticated. She served this mustard mousse with a peppery baked ham years ago at a brunch, and I never got over how great it looked (and tasted), shimmering away on a plate next to the platter of ham and a basket of biscuits. Here, it's terrific as a foil to the rich beef.

With a paper towel, rub the inside of a 5- to 6-cup decorative mold with oil and set aside.

Place ¼ cup of the water in a small bowl and sprinkle the gelatin over the surface. Set aside.

In a medium bowl, combine the sugar, dry mustard, turmeric, and celery salt. Whisk to break up any mustard lumps. Whisk in the eggs, one at a time, until thoroughly combined.

Pour the mixture into the top of a double boiler set over hot water on medium heat. Whisk in the gelatin mixture, the vinegar, and the remaining ¾ cup water. Continue whisking continuously until the gelatin has dissolved and the mixture thickens slightly. Remove from the heat.

Transfer the mixture to a medium bowl and chill until it mounds slightly when dropped from a spoon. Fold in the whipped cream and pour into the prepared mold. Cover with plastic wrap and refrigerate for 4 to 6 hours until set.

When ready to serve, dip the bottom of the mold into hot water for a few seconds and unmold onto a serving plate.

Wesson oil or similar neutral-tasting oil for oiling the mold

1 cup cold water

1 tablespoon (1 envelope Knox) unflavored gelatin

½ cup sugar

2 tablespoons dry mustard

¾ teaspoon ground turmeric

1 teaspoon celery salt

4 large eggs, at room temperature

½ cup apple cider vinegar

1 cup heavy cream, whipped to soft peaks

Horseradish Mousse

My mother makes her horseradish mousse with lemon Jell-O, mayonnaise, and heavy cream—a combo that tastes far better than it sounds. Mary Sferruzza (who gave me the mustard mousse recipe on page 151) makes a more purist version with unflavored gelatin and heavy cream. At a recent V.D. dinner, I served both, and my guests were split evenly down the middle. The version here is a compromise of sorts.

With a paper towel, rub the inside of a 4- to 5-cup decorative mold or small loaf pan with oil and set aside.

Place the water in a small saucepan and sprinkle the gelatin over the surface. Set aside for 5 minutes to soften. Then heat over low heat until the gelatin has dissolved. Set aside to cool.

In a small bowl, fold the mayonnaise into the whipped cream and then gently fold in the horseradish. Fold in the onion, salt, sugar, lemon juice and zest, and a pinch of white pepper. Stir in the gelatin mixture.

Pour the mayonnaise mixture into the prepared mold. Cover with plastic wrap and refrigerate for 4 to 6 hours until firm.

When ready to serve, dip the bottom of the mold into hot water for a few seconds and unmold onto a serving plate.

NOTE: *This mousse can be used in place of the horseradish sauce included in the A Christmas Cocktail Supper menu on page 177. Guests cut a tiny slice and top a piece of rare tenderloin they've already put on a warm yeast roll.*

Serves 16 as a condiment

Wesson oil or similar neutral-tasting oil for oiling the mold

¼ cup water

1 tablespoon (1 envelope Knox) unflavored gelatin

¼ cup Hellmann's mayonnaise

¾ cup heavy cream, whipped to soft peaks

1 cup prepared horseradish

2 tablespoons finely chopped onion

2 teaspoons salt

2 teaspoons sugar

2 teaspoons fresh lemon juice

1 teaspoon lemon zest

Freshly ground white pepper

Scalloped Oysters

Serves 8

6 ounces (1½ sticks) butter, plus more for the baking dish

2 pints shucked fresh oysters

2 sleeves Ritz crackers, unopened

¼ cup chopped Italian parsley leaves

⅓ cup thinly sliced celery (use the tenderest pale green hearts if you can)

½ cup thinly sliced scallions, including some of the tender green parts

2 teaspoons thyme leaves

2 teaspoons fresh lemon juice

1 teaspoon Lea & Perrins Worcestershire sauce

¾ cup heavy cream

Pinch of cayenne pepper

Salt and freshly ground black pepper

This is one of those dishes—a mainstay at holiday dinners and formal sit-downs—for which almost everybody in the Delta has a version. I've seen it made with saltine crackers and bread crumbs, but my mother, a Ritz cracker devotee, uses them exclusively. Like hers, most recipes don't call for much more than cream and oyster liquor, but I like mine with a bit more going on. This has only a few additions—celery, scallions, herbs, and lemon juice—so that the oyster flavor still shines. Some people add grated cheese on top, but I think that's going too far. I did try it with bread crumbs once, but who was I kidding? It is way better with the Ritz.

Preheat the oven to 425°F. Grease a 9 by 13-inch baking dish with butter (I usually use an oval gratin dish with roughly those same measurements, but a Pyrex casserole dish is also fine).

Drain the oysters in a strainer over a medium bowl, reserving 2 tablespoons of the oyster liquor. Lay out the oysters in a single layer on paper towels.

Roll up the unopened sleeves of the crackers in a dish towel and smash with a rolling pin until you have small pieces, about 2½ cups. (You can also do this in a food processor, but I like the irregular coarseness of the rolling pin method—plus it's quick.)

Melt 8 tablespoons of the butter in a large sauté pan over medium heat. Remove from the heat and toss the cracker crumbs in the butter until evenly coated. Stir in the parsley, remove the mixture to a medium bowl, and set aside.

Wipe out the sauté pan and melt the remaining 4 tablespoons butter over medium-high heat. Sauté the celery and scallions, stirring occasionally, for about 3 minutes. Stir in the thyme, lemon juice, and Worcestershire sauce and simmer for 30 seconds. Add the cream and reserved oyster liquor and bring to a boil. Stir in the cayenne. Remove from the heat.

On the bottom of the buttered baking dish, sprinkle ½ cup of the cracker crumbs. Place a layer of oysters on top of the crumbs and sprinkle lightly with salt and black pepper. Drizzle half the cream mixture on top. Repeat with 1 cup of the remaining cracker crumbs, the remaining oysters, and the remaining cream. Top with the remaining 1 cup cracker crumbs.

Bake until bubbling and the oysters are just cooked through, 15 to 20 minutes. Serve immediately.

Jason's Spinach

Serves 8

8 tablespoons (1 stick) butter

2 tablespoons olive oil

¾ cup finely chopped shallots

4 pounds baby spinach, washed and dried

1 teaspoon salt

Freshly ground black pepper

Freshly ground white pepper

1 teaspoon fresh lemon juice

My great friend Jason Epstein showed me how to make this spinach the same night he taught me to make his fabulous fried oyster hors d'oeuvres (see page 43). I like the texture so much better than that of sautéed spinach, and it's the perfect "dressy" spinach dish to have when a gratin would be too rich. The shallots provide a lovely sweetness, and while I adore lemon in almost everything, especially spinach, this is one time you need just a touch.

Melt the butter with the olive oil in a large deep sauté pan or Dutch oven over medium heat. Add the shallots and sauté until soft, about 3 minutes. Add the spinach, tossing continuously from the bottom of the pan. You may have to add the spinach in three or four batches, adding more as it wilts. When all the spinach has been added, put a lid on the pan for 1 to 2 minutes. Remove the lid and toss again, making sure all the spinach is coated in the butter and oil and the spinach is limp and shiny. Stir in the salt, generous lashings of black pepper and white pepper, and the lemon juice.

Remove the sautéed spinach from the heat. Taste for seasonings. You may need more salt or pepper, but this dish should not be too lemony.

Drain the spinach in a colander, discarding any liquid, and place in the bowl of a food processor fitted with a metal blade. Pulse a few times—you don't want the puree to be remotely runny or too smooth. The finished dish should be velvety but still maintain a bit of the texture of both the spinach and the shallots. Serve it in a covered silver vegetable dish or a bowl.

NOTE: *I've made this spinach ahead of time and reheated it in a heavy-bottomed pot over low heat. You could also put the spinach in a shallow buttered gratin dish, top it with a sprinkling of buttered bread crumbs, and reheat it in a 350°F oven for about 15 minutes, until warm all the way through.*

Consommé Rice Pilaf

Serves 8 to 10

Until recently, I'm pretty sure I hadn't eaten consommé rice in at least three decades. Likely invented in the Campbell's soup test kitchen along with the perennially popular green bean casserole, it was included at every church supper and country club buffet I ever went to as a child, and even at "fancy" dinners like this one. And then it vanished—at least out of my life. I can't remember what possessed me to try it again, but now I make it all the time, unapologetically. In my youth, cooks added things like slivered almonds or canned sliced mushrooms and water chestnuts. This version includes sautéed fresh mushrooms, which elevates things considerably.

Preheat the oven to 350°F.

Melt 6 tablespoons of the butter in a large skillet over medium-high heat. Add the onion, then reduce the heat to medium and cook until soft and slightly brown, 5 to 6 minutes. Add the rice and stir continuously for another 2 minutes.

Remove the rice mixture from the heat and transfer it to a large bowl. Stir in the consommé and set aside.

Wipe out the skillet and melt the remaining 2 tablespoons butter with the olive oil over high heat. Add the mushrooms, sprinkle with salt and pepper, and add a few healthy dashes of Worcestershire sauce. Toss and shake the pan for about 5 minutes, until the mushrooms are brown. Remove from the heat and stir the mushrooms into the rice mixture.

Turn the rice mixture into an ungreased soufflé dish, cover tightly with aluminum foil, and bake for 1 hour. Serve immediately.

- **8** tablespoons (1 stick) butter
- **1** large onion, finely chopped (about 1½ cups)
- **2** cups Uncle Ben's Original Converted rice
- **Three** 10½-ounce cans Campbell's beef consommé
- **2** tablespoons olive oil
- **1** pound white button or baby bella mushrooms, sliced
- Salt and freshly ground black pepper
- Lea & Perrins Worcestershire sauce

Charlotte Russe

Serves 8 to 10

½ cup whole milk

2 tablespoons (2 envelopes Knox) unflavored gelatin

1 quart heavy cream, plus whipped cream for garnish

1½ cups sugar

5 large eggs, separated

½ cup bourbon or brandy

About **24** ladyfingers, split apart

I included my mother's charlotte russe recipe in my very first food column for the *New York Times Magazine,* and it turned out to be the smartest move I could have made—it's so sinfully yummy that the recipe tester loved me from that moment on. This dessert is so easy but very grand and just right for a special occasion.

Place the milk in a small saucepan and sprinkle the gelatin over the surface. Set aside for 5 minutes to soften. Heat over low heat until the gelatin has dissolved. Set aside to cool.

In a large bowl, beat the heavy cream and 1 cup of the sugar with an electric mixer until firm peaks form when the beaters are raised. Set aside.

Place the egg yolks in a second large bowl and gradually beat in the remaining ½ cup sugar. Beat at high speed for several minutes, until the mixture is thick and pale yellow. Stir in the gelatin mixture and bourbon. With a rubber spatula, fold in one-quarter of the whipped cream to lighten the mixture. Then fold in the remaining whipped cream.

In another large bowl, using clean beaters, beat the egg whites until soft peaks form when the beaters are raised. Fold the egg whites into the cream mixture.

Line a deep trifle bowl with the ladyfingers, split sides facing inward. Spoon in the cream mixture, cover with plastic wrap, and chill in the refrigerator until set, 4 to 6 hours.

Decorate the charlotte russe with dollops of whipped cream on top.

NOTE: *This dessert is so festive that it seems to demand a little something in addition to the whipped cream. You could sprinkle the whipped cream clouds with crushed candied nuts or top them with fresh raspberries. When violets are blooming in my garden, I dip them in beaten egg white and then in superfine sugar and lay them on a plate to dry before placing them on top. When kumquats are in season, I slice them thin, simmer them in simple syrup for 20 minutes, and decorate with them instead.*

A JEFFERSONIAN EVENING

When Jon Meacham's *Thomas Jefferson: The Art of Power* was released in paperback, Jon came to New Orleans for a talk and a signing. Afterward, I organized a small dinner that would not only honor the author but also serve as an homage to his subject.

I'm hardly the first person to create a menu around Jefferson's many culinary passions. The gifted cook and historian, Damon Lee Fowler is the author of *Dining at Monticello,* and there's also *Thomas Jefferson's Cook Book* by Marie Kimball. Only eight recipes in Jefferson's own hand survive (including one for a beef stew and another for an almond cream), but there are diaries from his guests, his own detailed garden notes, a cookbook by a granddaughter, and, perhaps most important, records of the many foods he imported from Europe.

Jefferson's five years as U.S. minister in France were not lost on the worldly future president. While there, he arranged French cooking lessons for his slave James Hemings, and when he returned home, he brought with him eighty-six crates containing art and books, silver and porcelain, but also such necessities as olive oil, mustard, pasta, almonds, vinegar, and 680 bottles of wine. Until the day he died, he would order similar shipments. Just after the War of 1812, for example, a letter he wrote to the American consul to Marseilles included an analysis of Napoleon Bonaparte's downfall as well as a "declaration of wants." Just six months before his death in 1826, he authorized payment of freight and duties on what would be his last shipment from Marseille, and his final cellar inventory listed "virgin oil of Aix, anchovies, 112¾ lb Maccaroni."

Jefferson was also the original farm-to-table host. His fifty-seven years of garden notes contain entries like the one on April 24, 1767: "forwardest peas of Feb. 20. come to table." Fresh English peas were his first love—he held good-natured competitions with neighboring gentlemen farmers as to whose peas would be the earliest of the season, and he devoted the most space in his garden to them. In addition, he planted a wide variety of lettuces (including Brown Dutch, Tennis Ball, and Spotted Aleppo) eight times a year.

As in pretty much every household in Virginia, cured hams were always at the ready. So presumably was lamb, since he also raised sheep. At one point during his presidency, forty of them grazed in the square in front of the White House (a ram once gored to death an unsuspecting passerby).

At Monticello, Jefferson often read in the tea room while waiting for his family to gather for meals, and there were stacks of volumes atop the mantel. So it seemed fitting to stage our dinner in the same room as a Regency breakfront filled with books (including those by Jon, of course). To start, I chose crab Norfolk, in honor of the port through which most of Jefferson's foodstuffs arrived, as well as Virginia's copious bounty of blue crabs. A French-inspired lamb stew seemed appropriate, as did the "macaroni" that Jefferson introduced to America. The former president referred to all noodles as "macaroni," and one of his many White House guests described eating "a pie called macaroni" (though the unknowing fellow mistook the noodles for onions). Jefferson had a pasta machine at Monticello and ordered countless pounds of Parmesan cheese from Europe, so my own "pie," made from penne, is my tribute.

It goes without saying that a salad—with lots of peas, lettuces, and herbs—should be included, especially one with a mustardy vinaigrette. In April 1810, Jefferson wrote to his namesake grandson, "We are out of salad-oil, and you know it is a necessity of life here." He pronounced the oil from Aix the world's finest and preferred (as do I) the Dijon mustard produced by Maille.

Jefferson is often credited with bringing ice cream to America, but George Washington had an ice cream freezer at Mount Vernon and the colonial governor of Williamsburg offered ice cream as early as 1770. Jefferson certainly popularized ice cream, though, serving it at the White House in pastry shells, and writing out the first American recipe (made with six egg yolks,

"2 bottles of good cream," sugar, and vanilla) that now resides in the Library of Congress. In *Dining at Monticello*, the author conjectures that the pastry shells were akin to the cream puffs I filled with ice cream for my recipe in this menu. While there is no record of any chocolate sauce served with them, I couldn't resist. The Jefferson household was extremely fond of hot chocolate and invariably served it in a silver vessel—copied from an excavated Roman bronze *askos* (pouring vessel) Jefferson saw in France. The family nicknamed it "the duck," and it was ever present, so I offered up extra amounts of the chocolate sauce here in a similar silver pourer.

Jefferson was also the original farm-to-table host.

During dinner, we toasted Jon's well-deserved success with lots of "Jeffersonian" wine, in this case, a Gevrey-Chambertin. When he became president, Jefferson ordered one hundred dozen bottles of the stuff, making it the first (and likely the last) Grand Cru Burgundy ever served at the White House. One of Jefferson's granddaughters referred to Jefferson's many dinners as "Feasts of Reason." While I'm not sure we quite hit that mark, we had a feast nonetheless.

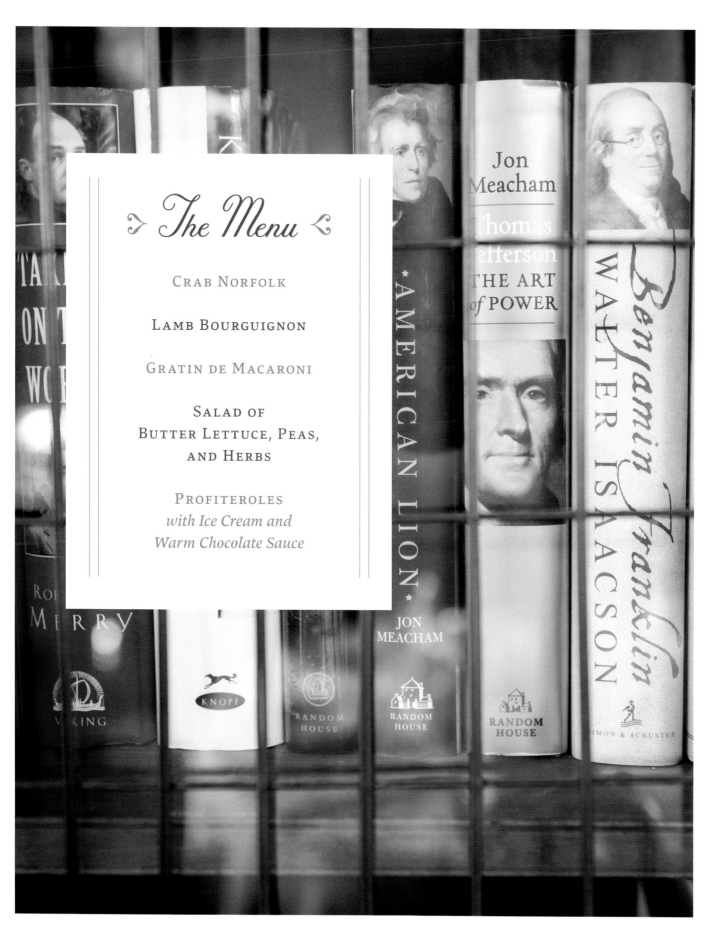

❧ The Menu ❧

Crab Norfolk

Lamb Bourguignon

Gratin de Macaroni

Salad of Butter Lettuce, Peas, and Herbs

Profiteroles
with Ice Cream and Warm Chocolate Sauce

A NOTE ON THE TABLE SETTING

At Monticello, Jefferson dined and entertained in both the dining and the tea rooms, always with monogrammed white damask linens (though the cloth came off after dinner when the nutmeats, fruit, and wine came in). While in Paris, Jefferson shipped home 120 plates, 2 soup tureens, and 5 large porcelain platters. Not much survives except for 2 serving pieces in the cornflower garland pattern made at the royal factory at Sèvres. The pattern was originally produced for one of Louis XVI's dining rooms at Versailles, and, thanks to my antiques dealer friends Peter Patout and Patrick Dunne, I managed to gather enough of those original cornflower plates for our dinner. (Herend makes a contemporary cornflower pattern.) When I married, Patrick, owner of Lucullus in New Orleans (see Sources, page 219), gave me six French forks and tablespoons in the same Fiddle and Thread pattern Jefferson used, and over the years, he's sold me a ton of heavy French stemware along the lines of the "39 footed glasses" Jefferson shipped to Monticello in 1790.

For the water glasses, it seemed fitting to use silver tumblers. Today's popular "Jefferson Cup" is based on a design with a round bottom and vermeil interior that the attentive Jefferson bought for himself in Paris. Years later, he asked a Richmond-based silversmith to make eight more of the cups, which often held beer, cider, and even after-dinner wine at Monticello dinners.

LITTLE MOUNTAIN BIG IDEAS

Keith asked William Dunlap, our dear friend, great artist, and all-round force of nature, to make this painting as her gift to Jon when *The Art of Power* was published. *Little Mountain Big Ideas* now hangs in Jon's office at home in Nashville, and I used the image to create our invitation to dinner. I have a similar work by Dunlap, *Jeffersonian Democracy: A Work in Progress*, which features Monticello—except that there are a bunch of hound dogs ravaging some watermelons in the foreground. Keith and I are both of the opinion that you can never have too many Dunlaps hanging around.

Crab Norfolk

*Serves 6
as a first course,
or 4
as a main dish*

1 pound jumbo lump crab-
meat

1 tablespoon fresh lemon
juice

6 slices white sandwich
bread, such as Pepper-
idge Farm

8 tablespoons (1 stick)
butter, plus softened
butter for the toast

¼ cup finely diced country
ham

2 tablespoons sherry

Pinch of salt

Tabasco sauce

According to Craig Claiborne, who included a crab Norfolk recipe in his 1987 book, *Craig Claiborne's Southern Cooking*, the dish was invented in Norfolk, Virginia, at the Snowden and Mason Restaurant in 1924. If Claiborne's right, country ham isn't original to the dish, but it certainly enhances it, and I've seen crispy bits of ham in at least a few versions. Shellfish and cured pork have long had an affinity for each other (think clams casino), and country ham certainly abounds in Virginia, so the combo makes perfect sense.

Preheat the oven to 450°F.

Place the crabmeat in a bowl and gently pick over the lumps to remove any trace of shell or cartilage. Sprinkle with the lemon juice.

Trim the bread crusts and spread each slice with softened butter on both sides. Place the slices on a baking sheet. Bake for 8 to 10 minutes, turning once, so that both sides are golden brown.

Meanwhile, melt the of butter in a large skillet over medium-high heat. Add the ham and sauté, stirring continuously for 3 to 4 minutes, until the bits are slightly crisp. Lower the heat to medium and add the crabmeat. Sprinkle in the sherry, a generous pinch of salt, and 3 or 4 drops of Tabasco. Gently stir, leaving the lumps as large as possible, while making sure the ham is incorporated throughout. Cook only until the crabmeat is heated through, and taste to see if more salt, lemon, or Tabasco is needed.

Slice each piece of toast in half and line up on individual dessert or salad plates. Spoon a serving of the crabmeat mixture on top of each toast half.

Lamb Bourguignon

Serves 8

4 to 5 pounds boneless
  lamb shoulder, cut into
  2-inch cubes

2½ teaspoons kosher salt,
  plus more for season-
  ing

1 teaspoon freshly ground
  black pepper, plus
  more for seasoning

1 medium carrot, diced,
  plus ½ pound, sliced

1 celery stalk, diced

1 large yellow onion, plus
  1 medium, diced

4 juniper berries, crushed

2 whole cloves, crushed

1 bay leaf and a few thyme,
  parsley, and tarragon
  sprigs, tied together
  with kitchen twine to
  make a bouquet garni

1 orange zest strip, about ¾
  inch wide and 3 inches
  long

1 bottle full-bodied young
  red wine, such as
  Burgundy or Côtes du
  Rhône

6 tablespoons olive oil

4 ounces pancetta or thick-
  cut bacon, cut into
  small dice

6 garlic cloves, minced

2 tablespoons tomato
  paste

(continued)

This dish is based on a lamb daube recipe from Mark Peel, the gifted owner/chef of Los Angeles's late and much-lamented Campanile. I love the vaguely orange-scented daubes of southern France and, like Julie and Julia and pretty much everyone else in the world, I am crazy about a classic beef bourguignon. This recipe is sort of a combination of the two. I use lamb here because Jefferson raised lambs, but also because I love the deep, rich flavor the meat imparts to the stew. Also, if possible, it's worth both marinating the lamb for the full forty-eight hours ahead of time and cooking the stew itself at least one day before serving. When I do both, I can really tell the difference in the flavor.

At least one day before you plan to cook the stew, place the lamb cubes in a large bowl or deep-sided pot and season generously with salt and pepper.

In another large bowl, mix together the diced carrot, celery, large onion, juniper berries, cloves, bouquet garni, 1 teaspoon of the salt, the pepper, orange zest, and red wine. Pour the marinade over the lamb and mix well. Cover and refrigerate for 12 to 48 hours, turning the lamb cubes two or three times.

Remove the lamb from the marinade, scrape the vegetables and spices back into the pot, and blot the lamb pieces dry with paper towels. Transfer the lamb to a clean large bowl. Season with salt and pepper and set aside.

Drain the marinade through a colander set over a bowl and reserve the liquid, the vegetables, and the bouquet garni separately, and set aside.

Heat 2 tablespoons of the olive oil in a large heavy-bottomed pot over high heat. Brown the lamb cubes on all sides in batches, adding more oil if necessary. With a slotted spoon, transfer the browned lamb to a clean large bowl.

Pour off the fat from the pot, turn the heat to medium, and add the pancetta. When the pancetta begins to render its fat, add the vegetables from the marinade, stirring to deglaze the bottom of the pan. Add the garlic and cook until the vegetables soften, about 5 minutes. Stir in the tomato paste and cook for about 2 minutes more. Stir in the reserved liquid from the marinade and the chicken or lamb stock and bring to a boil, stirring occasionally and scraping the bottom of the pot with a wooden spoon. Add the lamb and any juices that have accumulated in the bowl, along with the bouquet garni from the marinade and 1 teaspoon of the remaining salt. Bring to a simmer and skim off the foam that rises to the surface. Cover the pot and cook for 2 hours.

1 cup chicken stock or Homemade Lamb Stock (page 22)

2 leeks, rinsed, drained, and sliced, including the tender green part

2 tablespoons butter

1 pound white button mushrooms, left whole if small, halved or quartered if large, and brushed clean

Lea & Perrins Worcestershire sauce

Remove the lamb from the pot and place in a large bowl or the saucepan in which you'll finish the stew. Strain the liquid through a strainer set over a medium bowl. Discard the bouquet garni and push on the vegetables so that a portion goes through the strainer into the liquid. (If serving the next day, cover and refrigerate the lamb and the broth separately overnight, then discard the fat that has solidified on the top of the broth. If serving the same day, allow the broth to rest for 30 minutes and skim off the fat with a spoon.)

When you are ready to serve, bring the stew to a boil in a large saucepan over medium-high heat, then reduce the heat to maintain a low simmer.

In a large skillet, heat 2 tablespoons of the olive oil over medium heat and add the diced onion, the sliced carrots, the leeks, and the remaining ½ teaspoon salt. Sauté, stirring often, for 10 minutes. Add the vegetables to the pot with the stew and simmer for 30 minutes.

Meanwhile, wipe out the skillet and heat the remaining 2 tablespoons oil and the butter over high heat. Add the mushrooms, season with salt and pepper, and sprinkle on a few dashes of Worcestershire sauce. Toss and shake the pan for about 5 minutes, until the mushrooms are brown, and add to the stew. Taste and season with additional salt and pepper, if needed.

Gratin de Macaroni

Serves 6 to 8

Butter for greasing the gratin dish

½ pound penne pasta

1½ cups crème fraîche

1½ cups whole milk

1 cup grated Gruyère cheese

¼ cup finely chopped Italian parsley leaves

½ teaspoon kosher salt

Freshly ground black pepper

2 tablespoons grated Parmesan cheese

My mother used to make a noodle casserole with egg noodles, butter, sour cream, lemon juice, and Parmesan. Neither of us can find that exact recipe, but I discovered something similar in—of all places—an out-of-print book on French bistros. This is much lighter and far speedier than a proper macaroni and cheese made with a béchamel sauce, and I prefer it, especially with daubes and stews. Feel free to get creative with the cheeses. I like the way the Parmesan browns on the top, but I've substituted everything from Cabot Clothbound Cheddar to Thomasville tomme (a buttery Pyrenees-style cow's-milk cheese from Georgia's Sweet Grass Dairy) for the Gruyère.

Preheat the oven to 425°F. Butter a shallow glass or earthenware gratin dish or casserole.

Cook the penne in boiling salted water according to the directions on the box. Drain and place in a large bowl. Fold in the crème fraîche, milk, and Gruyère. Stir in the parsley, salt, and pepper, and taste for seasonings.

Spread the mixture in the prepared dish and sprinkle with the Parmesan. Bake for 25 minutes, or until the cheese is browned on top and the liquid has been completely absorbed. Let sit for 5 minutes before serving.

Salad of Butter Lettuce,
Peas, and Herbs

Serves 8

Kosher salt

1 cup fresh or frozen peas

2 heads butter (also called Boston) lettuce, leaves separated

8 radishes, trimmed and thinly sliced

2 shallots thinly sliced, or 1 bunch scallions, white and light green parts only, thinly sliced

Sherry Mustard Vinaigrette (ingredients follow)

¼ cup mint leaves

¼ cup Italian parsley leaves

2 tablespoons tarragon leaves, very roughly chopped

2 tablespoons chives, snipped into ¼- to ½-inch pieces

Flaky sea salt, like Maldon

Freshly ground black pepper

You can make this salad exactly as is or use it as a guide. Because butter (also called Boston) lettuce is easily found in supermarkets—and because it closely resembles the Tennis Ball variety grown by Jefferson—I include it here, but you can (and should) substitute the second head with something seasonal from your local farmers' market or perhaps a bunch of watercress (with much of the stems removed). Jefferson's favorite herb was tarragon, but dill, fennel fronds, or basil would all be fine additions or substitutions. When I can find chervil, I substitute it for the parsley. The main thing is to make like Jefferson and pick what looks lively and fresh from the garden.

Bring a small pot of salted water to a boil over high heat. Add the peas and cook until just tender, no more than 2 to 3 minutes for fresh and less than that for frozen. Drain and set aside.

In a large bowl, toss the lettuce, radishes, shallots, and peas with enough of the vinaigrette to lightly coat. Add the mint, parsley, tarragon, and chives. Taste and add sea salt and pepper if needed.

Sherry Mustard Vinaigrette

Use a whisk to combine the lemon juice, vinegar, and mustard in a small bowl. Season lightly with salt and pepper. Slowly add 6 tablespoons of the olive oil, whisking continuously. Taste and add more oil, salt, and pepper, as needed.

1 tablespoon fresh lemon
juice

1 tablespoon good red
wine vinegar or sherry
vinegar

1 tablespoon Dijon mustard, preferably Maille

Kosher salt and freshly
ground black pepper

6 to **8** tablespoons
extra-virgin olive oil

Profiteroles with Chocolate Sauce

1 cup water

8 tablespoons (1 stick) unsalted butter

Kosher salt

1 cup all-purpose flour

4 large eggs

1 pint Talenti toasted almond gelato, or ice cream of your choice

Chocolate Sauce

P rofiteroles are a prime example of things that look hard but are really very simple to make. Because Jefferson was known for importing almonds, I used Talenti's delicious toasted almond gelato to fill these.

Preheat the oven to 425°F. Line a pair of cookie sheets with parchment paper and set aside.

Combine the water, butter, and a pinch of salt in a heavy-bottomed saucepan and bring to a boil over high heat. Add the flour all at once and beat with a wooden spoon until the mixture comes together and forms a sticky ball at the bottom of the pan. Lower the heat and continue to cook, stirring constantly, for 2 minutes.

Remove the mixture from the heat and add the eggs, one at a time, beating to make sure each egg is fully incorporated. (You can also place the mixture in the bowl of a food processor fitted with the metal blade, pulsing after the addition of each egg.) The dough should be thick and shiny.

Spoon the dough into a pastry bag fitted with a large plain round tip and pipe it into rounds about 2 inches in diameter and 1 inch high on the prepared cookie sheets. (You can use a Ziploc bag with a corner snipped off, or you can form the mounds with two soupspoons.) Wet the tip of your finger and smooth the pointy tops of each mound. You should have 18 to 24 mounds.

Bake the puffs for 10 minutes. Reduce the heat and bake until the puffs are golden brown and completely firm, about 20 minutes more. Cool on a wire rack to room temperature.

When ready to serve, cut off the tops of the puffs and set the lids aside. Fill the puffs with ice cream and place the lid of each puff over the filling. (At this point, you can freeze the filled puffs for up to 2 hours.) Arrange the puffs in a large serving bowl. Drizzle with warm chocolate sauce and serve at once.

14 ounces semisweet or bittersweet chocolate, broken into pieces

2 tablespoons butter

¼ cup sugar

¾ cup heavy cream

Pinch of salt

Chocolate Sauce

Combine the chocolate, butter, sugar, and cream in a heavy-bottomed saucepan and melt together over very low heat, stirring continuously.

Remove from the heat, add the salt, and whisk until the mixture comes together smoothly.

A CHRISTMAS COCKTAIL SUPPER

A cocktail supper, a wildly popular form of entertaining in the Mississippi Delta, is essentially a big boozy bash with more than enough food to constitute supper. It's not called a cocktail party because the offerings extend well beyond passed canapés (though they are on offer), and it's not called a buffet supper because silverware and plates aren't required (though sometimes I'll put out stacks of small plates along with cocktail napkins). Its magic lies in the fact that even the more substantial menu items are designed to be consumed easily and relatively neatly with your hands, so that the more crucial business of the evening—talking, laughing, drinking, flirting, moving toward someone you want to catch up with, moving away from someone you're trying to avoid—is not impeded by the pesky tasks of fixing a plate and sussing out a seat.

My mother is a huge proponent of the cocktail supper, and when I was growing up, she gave at least two or three during the holidays, including one on Christmas night. Though she and I both give them throughout the year, the format is an especially good marriage of party and season. For one thing, the halls are already decked and people are generally more primed to make merry. A big bowl of self-serve holiday punch gives the bartenders at least a bit of relief, and though I rarely offer sweets at these sorts of events, the bourbon balls featured here are too festive—and too delicious—not to pile up on the sideboard. (I

sometimes also fill little gift bags with them for guests to take home.)

Over the years, I've tweaked my mother's menu only slightly. On the dining room table, there's always a chafing dish filled with some sort of shellfish concoction, usually seafood Newburg or the crabmeat Mornay on this menu, as well as a platter of sliced rare tenderloin accompanied by warm yeast rolls, horseradish sauce, and homemade hot mustard. The latter (which may or may not have originated with a woman we referred to as Granny Lake, the formidable mother-in-law of my mother's close friend

Emma Jean) is something I've encountered only in the Delta. No matter where it came from, the sauce is now so entrenched that its absence is cause for alarm. A few years ago, at a christening party in Manhattan, I overheard a horrified exchange between a pair of Delta ladies: "Oh my God," said one to the other, "that mustard came from a jar."

In a bow to something green, there's a platter of steamed asparagus with curry dip, a mildly spicy mayonnaise-based mixture, that, like the mustard, I've been served only in the Delta. A second chafing dish contains a rich duck étouffée, which has Louisiana roots, of course. The New Orleans restaurant Upperline has a terrific version on their menu, and years ago it was served as an appetizer (with a dab of pepper jelly) on little corn pancakes like the ones on page 19. In the past, I passed a similar canapé, but for this party I arranged all my demitasse cups and spoons alongside the chafing dish so that guests could help themselves. I love those pretty cups, but I don't think I've ever used them for their intended purpose—my friends tend to stick with wine after dinner or move on to something stronger. Also, at that point, their hostess has no intention of making coffee! So it's fun to put the cups to use—the étouffée recipe is on page 206, and when I serve it this way, I thin it with a tiny bit more stock. Merry, merry!

The Menu

FROZEN WHISKEY SOURS

CHEESE DREAMS

MINI CORN MUFFINS
*with Smoked Salmon
and Dill Crème Fraîche*

DEVILED HAM GOUGÈRES

ASPARAGUS
with Curry Dip

CRABMEAT MORNAY
with Toast Points

DUCK ÉTOUFFÉE DEMITASSE

BEEF TENDERLOIN
*with Yeast Rolls, Hot Mustard,
and Horseradish Sauce*

BOURBON BALLS

A NOTE ON THE DECOR

In Louisiana, the holiday season coincides with citrus season, so it seems mad not to put all that gorgeous bounty to use. I wire my wreaths with satsuma oranges and/or Meyer lemons, and I decorated my first New Orleans tree with nothing but silver balls and kumquats threaded with hooks. Since then, I've gotten a lot more ambitious about the tree—the one pictured here is loaded with forty-five strings of white lights and countless ornaments consisting mostly of glass birds and other creatures that might nest there in real life. But the citrus remains the focus, not least because it looks so much more right in our mild-weather setting than heavily flocked trees or piles of pinecones. After all, Decembers can be so warm here that cedar or fir garland hung outdoors turns immediately brown—as you can see, I hang mine inside instead.

When we lived on First Street, I flanked the front door with some heavily laden Meyer lemon trees (I also like to bring at least one or two potted trees inside). My good friend Joan Griswold, an extraordinarily talented painter of interiors and still lifes, made me a painting of one of the lemons from those trees as a present, and it now hangs in my kitchen. For this party, I thought it especially fitting to use the image on the invitation. In this neck of the woods, a lemon (or orange or kumquat) is at least as much of a seasonal symbol as a poinsettia (and one that I prefer far more) and it was a pleasure to share Joan's lovely gift with our friends.

Frozen Whiskey Sours

My lifelong close friend Elizabeth Cordes is the queen of the frozen cocktail. During holiday time, she keeps these slushy bourbon sours at the ready in gallon-size Ziploc bags, a habit for which I was especially grateful a few years ago when I hosted an impromptu holiday shindig. I'd made a quick trip to Mississippi and was racing back to New Orleans in time to meet some friends of friends (and their children) from England and Spain at our house for drinks. Unwrapped presents were stacked everywhere, and there was almost no food left in the house. But the tree was pretty and still standing, and I knew we'd have swell music—just behind me on the highway were my great pals Eden Brent and her boyfriend (now husband) Bob Dowell, who plays a mean trombone. From the road, I invited a handful of neighbors, my husband's daughter and son-in-law, and Elizabeth, whose magic mix was sure to get things off the ground. It turned out to be one of our best parties ever. We talked and drank and danced and sang until finally, around eleven, somebody noticed that the kids were hungry and we ordered pizza from Domino's. Refueled, we kept at it until well after midnight.

Until then, at "official" holiday parties, I'd served such seasonal fare as eggnog or Champagne punch, but inspired by the memory of that festive evening, I now fill the punch bowl with the frozen sours instead. Anyway, as my mother continues to remind me, eggnog is strictly a morning drink.

Place the whiskey, orange juice, lemon juice, and sugar in a large bowl (I usually have to resort to a stockpot) and stir vigorously to dissolve the sugar. Dump in one jar of the cherries with their juice and mix well. With a strainer over a medium bowl, strain the rest of the cherries and reserve the juice. Add the cherries to the whiskey mixture and sweeten to taste with the remaining cherry juice.

Mix well and pour into a large plastic container (a big Tupperware bowl, a couple of pitchers, or the aforementioned Ziploc bags will work). Cover and freeze until slushy (it actually never freezes hard).

Serve the mixture in a punch bowl, making sure some of the cherries rise to the top. Float a few orange slices on top as well, dotting them in the center with a cherry.

Serves about 32

- **3** fifths bourbon whiskey, such as Maker's Mark
- **2** quarts fresh orange juice
- **2** cups fresh lemon juice
- **2** cups sugar
- **Four** 10-ounce jars maraschino cherries
- **1** orange, thinly sliced, for garnish

Cheese Dreams

Years ago, my dear friend Helen Bransford and I had a cocktail party in Nashville, and we begged Ernestine Turner, my grandmother's beloved cook, and Martha Wilhoite, my aunt's equally beloved cook and companion, to help us with the hors d'oeuvres. I had heard of cheese dreams, but they were like some magical, mythical entity—talked about in rhapsodic tones but never seen or tasted. The dinners Ernestine prepared for my grandparents at least five nights a week were insanely delicious (and almost hilariously formal), but they had long since quit having parties by the time I came along, and my aunt invariably entertained at the Belle Meade Country Club. But that night at Helen's house, both Ernestine and Martha could show off their party repertoires, whipping up a batch of the elusive cheese dreams with no recipe, talking (about everything but the business at hand) the whole time. Because I knew something important was happening, I tried to pay attention in between my own duties, and I still can't believe I never got either cook to write a recipe down. It has taken me more than twenty years, but I think I've gotten close to their creation. There are wildly varying recipes for cheese dreams in both *Nashville Seasons* and *The Memphis Cookbook* (produced by the Junior League in each city), but this version, I have to say, is better than the ones I've found in print, and dreamy indeed.

Makes
30 to 40 canapés

- ½ pound (2 sticks) butter, softened
- ½ pound sharp Cheddar cheese, grated (about 2 cups)
- 2 tablespoons heavy cream
- 1 large egg
- ½ teaspoon salt
- ½ teaspoon dry mustard
- 1 teaspoon Lea & Perrins Worcestershire sauce
- Generous pinch of cayenne pepper, or a couple dashes of Tabasco sauce
- 1 loaf firm white sandwich bread, such as Pepperidge Farm

Preheat the oven to 375°F. Line a baking sheet with parchment paper.

Cream the butter and Cheddar in the bowl of a stand mixer fitted with the whisk attachment. Add the cream, egg, salt, dry mustard, and Worcestershire sauce and mix well. Add the cayenne to taste and blend.

Cut the crusts off the bread slices, cut the bread into rectangles, and cut in half again. Make a "sandwich" of 2 squares by spreading some of the cheese mixture between them. Spread the cheese on top of each sandwich and spread a thin film around all four sides.

Place the sandwiches, bottom-side down, on the prepared cookie sheet. Bake for 15 minutes or until golden brown.

NOTE: *These can be assembled the day before the party and kept refrigerated on the baking sheet. They can also be frozen before baking—freeze them on the baking sheet until they're hard, then place them in Ziploc freezer bags. Pop them into the oven straight from the freezer, but allow for a longer baking time.*

Mini Corn Muffins
with Smoked Salmon and Dill Crème Fraîche

Makes about 36 canapés

Butter for greasing the muffin cups

One 8½-ounce can cream-style corn

1 cup white cornmeal

1 cup sour cream

2 tablespoons vegetable oil

1½ teaspoons baking powder

1 teaspoon salt

2 large eggs

1 cup crème fraîche

2 tablespoons finely chopped dill, plus 1 bunch sprigs for garnish

1 tablespoon fresh lemon juice

Freshly ground black pepper

½ pound thinly sliced smoked salmon

When I lived on Manhattan's Upper East Side, I was half a block from Butterfield Market, which had superlative smoked salmon and the most amazing Danish brown bread ever. For parties, I invariably spread fingers of the bread with dill butter and made smoked salmon canapés, but once I moved south (and far away from the beloved Butterfield), I replaced the brown bread with corn bread mini muffins and the butter with dill crème fraîche.

Preheat the oven to 350°F. Generously grease 36 mini-muffin cups with butter and set aside.

Place the corn, cornmeal, sour cream, vegetable oil, baking powder, salt, and eggs in a large bowl and mix well. Transfer to a blender or the bowl of a food processor and process for a minute or less, until the mixture is smooth.

Fill each muffin cup about halfway with the batter. Bake for 20 minutes, or until the muffins are golden brown on top. Remove from the oven and place the tins on a rack to cool.

Meanwhile, in a small bowl, combine the crème fraîche, chopped dill, and lemon juice and stir to mix well. Fold in pepper to taste.

Cut the muffins in half and smear each side with ¼ to ½ teaspoon of the crème fraîche mixture. Depending on the width of the salmon slices, you'll need to cut or tear each slice into thirds or quarters—you want a piece big enough to hang over the muffin slightly. (If I'm feeling generous, I'll fold a larger slice in half—you'll know what to do.) Place the salmon on the bottom half of each muffin. Top with a dill sprig (it looks pretty if the sprig sticks out a bit) and place the muffin tops on top.

Deviled Ham Gougères

I love deviled ham, especially at Christmastime, when there's usually a bit of country ham around to add to the mix. It's good on finger sandwiches; it's good with crackers. But I especially love it stuffed into cheese gougères, savory choux paste puffs that I think are vastly overlooked as delivery systems for all kinds of yummy fillings.

Preheat the oven to 425°F. Line two baking sheets with parchment paper.

Combine the water, butter, and salt in a heavy-bottomed saucepan and bring to a boil over high heat. Add the flour all at once and beat with a wooden spoon until the mixture comes together and forms a sticky ball at the bottom of the pan. Lower the heat and continue to cook, stirring continuously, for 2 minutes.

Remove from the heat and add the eggs, one at a time, beating with a wooden spoon to make sure each egg is fully incorporated. (You can also place the dough in the bowl of a food processor fitted with a metal blade. Add the eggs, one at a time, and pulse after each addition.) The mixture should be thick and shiny. Add the Gruyère and stir until well blended.

Fill a pastry bag fitted with large plain round tip with the mixture and pipe 1-inch-diameter rounds 1 inch apart onto the baking sheets. Alternatively, spoon level tablespoons (about the size of a cherry tomato) 1 inch apart. Sprinkle with the Parmesan. Bake for 10 minutes. Lower the oven temperature to 375°F and bake until puffed, golden, and crisp, about 20 minutes more. Remove from the oven and let cool before filling.

TO MAKE THE DEVILED HAM

Combine the ham and onion in the bowl of a food processor fitted with a metal blade and chop finely. Add the mustard, mayonnaise, sweet pickles, horseradish, Worcestershire sauce, and cayenne and blend well.

To fill the gougères, make a small slit in the side of each puff. Scrape the deviled ham into a pastry bag or plastic Ziploc bag with the corner cut off. Squeeze some of the filling into each gougère and serve on a platter or passing tray.

NOTE: *If you have country ham on hand, use half country ham and half regular.*

Makes about 36 canapés

1 cup water

8 tablespoons (1 stick) butter, cut into tablespoons

½ teaspoon salt

1 cup all-purpose flour

4 large eggs

6 ounces Gruyère cheese, grated (about 1½ cups)

2 to 3 tablespoons grated Parmesan cheese

FOR THE DEVILED HAM

1 pound cooked ham, cut into approximately 1-inch cubes

½ cup roughly chopped onion

½ cup Dijon mustard

¼ cup Hellmann's mayonnaise

3 tablespoons chopped sweet pickles or chow-chow

1 teaspoon prepared horseradish

1 teaspoon Lea & Perrins Worcestershire sauce

Pinch of cayenne pepper

Asparagus with Curry Dip

3 to 4 pounds asparagus
Salt
Curry Dip

Makes about 2¼ cups

2 cups Hellmann's mayonnaise
2 tablespoons Durkee Famous Sauce
2 tablespoons Heinz ketchup
1 tablespoon curry powder
1 tablespoon prepared horseradish
1 tablespoon Lea & Perrins Worcestershire sauce
2 teaspoons grated white onion
1 teaspoon celery seeds
1 teaspoon Tabasco sauce
1 garlic clove, pressed
Salt

Most people serve curry dip with a platter of raw crudités, but I prefer it with steamed asparagus. Not only are the colors gorgeous together, the tastes are weirdly simpatico as well. Frankly, there is nothing I don't like with curry dip. Be sure to make enough to have on sandwiches with the leftover tenderloin, and it's also great with cold roast lamb and chicken.

Snap off the tough ends of the asparagus and discard.

Bring a large pot of water to a boil over high heat. Add a generous pinch of salt and the asparagus. Return the water to a boil and cook until the asparagus are tender, 3 to 5 minutes. Drain the asparagus and spread the spears out on a cookie sheet lined with paper towels or a dish towel.

Serve the asparagus alongside a bowl of curry dip.

NOTE: *If need be, you can refrigerate the asparagus for a few hours ahead of time, but roll them in dish towels or paper towels before putting them in a Ziploc bag or container, and don't keep them overnight—they'll get too watery.*

Curry Dip

In a medium bowl, combine the mayonnaise, Durkee sauce, ketchup, curry powder, horseradish, Worcestershire sauce, onion, celery seeds, Tabasco, and garlic. Stir in a pinch of salt and adjust the salt and curry powder to taste. Cover and refrigerate for up to 3 days, until ready to use.

NOTE: *The Durkee sauce is not crucial to this recipe, but if you can find it, add it.*

Crabmeat Mornay
with Toast Points

I adapted this yummy recipe years ago from one in *Bayou Cuisine,* produced by the churchwomen of St. Stephen's Episcopal Church in Indianola, Mississippi. While at this party, it's served in a chafing dish, it also makes a lovely passed hors d'oeuvre when spooned into mini tart shells. For the latter, I try and find Siljans croustades on the grocer's shelf or Athens mini filo shells in the freezer case.

Melt the butter in a large heavy-bottomed saucepan over medium-high heat. Add the scallions and sauté for about 3 minutes, until soft. Whisk in the flour. Add the cream and whisk until smooth. Stir in the Gruyère and blend until smooth. Add the sherry, cayenne, and salt. Gently fold in the crabmeat and parsley. Taste for seasonings. Serve the crab in a chafing dish accompanied by toast points.

Toast Points

Preheat the oven to 250°F.

Cut the crusts off the bread and cut each slice in half diagonally. Line up the trimmed bread on a baking sheet.

Bake until the bread is completely hard, about 30 minutes. The bread should be only barely colored.

NOTE: *You can store the toast points in Ziploc bags or cookie tins for at least a week.*

Serves about 30 as an hors d'oeuvre

8 tablespoons (1 stick) butter

1 bunch scallions, chopped, with some green tops included

2 tablespoons all-purpose flour

2 cups heavy cream

8 ounces Gruyère cheese, grated (about 2 cups)

1 tablespoon dry sherry

¼ teaspoon cayenne pepper

¼ teaspoon salt

1 pound jumbo lump or lump crabmeat

½ cup chopped Italian parsley leaves

Toast Points

Makes 32 toast points

16 slices firm white sandwich bread, such as Pepperidge Farm

Beef Tenderloin with
Hot Mustard and Horseradish Sauce

Makes 24 to 36 sandwiches

One 5- to 7-pound whole beef tenderloin, trimmed

4 tablespoons (½ stick) butter, softened

Kosher salt and freshly ground black pepper

Hot Mustard (recipe follows)

Horseradish Sauce (recipe follows)

36 yeast rolls, such as Sister Schubert's rolls, warm from the oven

I don't think my mother has ever had a cocktail supper that didn't include rare tenderloin and yeast rolls, so when I got to New York, I was astonished to discover tenderloin being offered up on tasteless, room-temperature hard rolls. For years, Mama—and everybody else—had to make her own yeast rolls, but now it's as easy as stopping by the supermarket freezer case or going online to Sister Schubert's (see Sources, page 219). Sister's rolls are almost as pillowy and buttery as the homemade kind (they are "homemade" in her industrial kitchen in Alabama) and are an excellent accompaniment to the beef, I assure you. To gild the lily, brush the rolls with melted butter just before they come out of the oven.

Preheat the oven to 425°F.

Place the beef in a shallow roasting pan and rub with the butter, making sure to cover completely. Sprinkle generously with salt and pepper. (I have a pepper grinder with an especially coarse grind—if you have one, too, use it.)

Bake for 25 minutes, or until a meat thermometer inserted into the thickest portion registers 125°F for rare meat. (Cook longer according to taste, but it's sort of a crime to cook this past 135°F.) Cover loosely with aluminum foil and let stand for at least 15 minutes before slicing.

Serve the tenderloin on a platter, alongside a basket of yeast rolls and bowls of homemade hot mustard and horseradish sauce.

NOTE: *When I serve tenderloin at dinner parties, I cut the meat into generous 1-inch slices. For parties like this one, where the meat is served on rolls, ½-inch slices are best.*

Hot Mustard

Makes 2¼ cups

1 cup dry mustard, such as Colman's

1 cup apple cider vinegar

1 cup sugar

3 large eggs, beaten well

Whisk together the dry mustard and vinegar in a medium stainless steel bowl. Cover and allow to soak overnight at room temperature.

In the bottom of a double boiler, bring about 2 inches of water to a boil over high heat. Lower the heat to maintain a steady simmer and add the mustard mixture to the top part of the pan. Add the sugar and eggs, stirring continuously until the mixture thickens. Remove from the heat to cool to room temperature.

When the mixture has cooled, refrigerate, covered with plastic wrap, for at least 2 hours or overnight. When just off the stove, the mixture will have the consistency of a thick soup, but it will thicken considerably when refrigerated.

NOTE: *This mustard is also really delicious with ham.*

Horseradish Sauce

Place the horseradish, sour cream, heavy cream, mustard, lemon juice, salt, and sugar in a medium bowl and fold to combine. Check for seasoning (you may want to add more salt and/or lemon juice) and stir in pepper to taste.

Makes about 2 cups

6 tablespoons prepared horseradish

1⅓ cups sour cream

½ cup heavy cream, whipped to soft peaks

1½ teaspoons Dijon mustard

2 teaspoons fresh lemon juice

1 teaspoon salt

½ teaspoon sugar

Freshly ground black pepper

Bourbon Balls

James Beard called these boozy morsels Spirit Balls, but by any name they are addictive, and, like Divinity, they always remind me of Christmas. Traditionally, they are rolled in confectioners' sugar, but I also roll them in crushed, toasted, and salted pecans. The recipe calls for plain pecans in the balls themselves, but on the outside, the crunchier salty pecans are a great match with the chocolate.

Place the wafers in a blender or the bowl of a food processor fitted with the metal blade and pulverize to a fine crumb.

In a large bowl, combine the crumbs with the cocoa powder, confectioners' sugar, pecans, corn syrup, and bourbon and mix well. Form into 1-inch balls and roll in confectioners' sugar.

NOTE: *Stored in an airtight container and refrigerated, the balls will keep for up to 2 weeks.*

Makes about 36 balls

One 12-ounce box Nabisco Nilla Wafers

2 tablespoons cocoa powder

1 cup confectioners' sugar, plus more for rolling

1 cup finely chopped pecans

2 tablespoons light corn syrup

½ cup bourbon

DUCK DINNER AT HOLLYWOOD PLANTATION

We held this dinner at Hollywood Plantation, a spectacular Greek Revival structure that appears like an apparition in the midst of hundreds of acres of soybeans and cotton in Benoit, Mississippi, about twenty miles north of Greenville. Built by Judge J. C. Burrus from 1858 to 1861, the house was spared destruction by the Yankees, thanks to the fact that the commander of the Union troops in the area had befriended the judge while at the University of Virginia. During the war, it became a makeshift hospital for hundreds of Confederate troops; after Lee's surrender, General Jubal Early hid out there before being secretly transported across the Mississippi by his host.

While that is some fascinating history indeed, most folks, me included, are more interested in the fact that the structure and surrounding grounds served as the location for the 1956 film *Baby Doll,* a mash-up of two Tennessee Williams one-act plays, *27 Wagons Full of Cotton* and *The Long Stay Cut Short,* that

starred Karl Malden, Carroll Baker, and Eli Wallach in his very first film role. The movie was billed as "Elia Kazan's production of Tennessee Williams' boldest story," with the "boldest" part driven home by its poster, featuring the twenty-five-year-old Baker (in the title role) wearing what is now universally known as a baby doll nightgown, curled up in a crib and rather provocatively sucking her thumb.

Not surprisingly, the movie gave rise to a new moniker the "Baby Doll House," but for decades the place was left to languish. Thankfully, a few years ago, the "Baby Doll House" was restored by the heirs of Judge Burrus's, including my pal Eustace Winn, who runs it as an event space and lives on the property, where he also farms.

In the hours before our dinner, we lived through about a week's worth of typically dramatic Delta weather. Just after a sunny arrival, a storm blew open the front door, sending tennis ball–size hailstones rolling through the center hall, while tornadoes touched down nearby. Thirty minutes later, a seriously perfect rainbow arced across the sky. Needless to say, the afternoon duck hunters returned empty-handed, but we already had far more than we needed: music and dancing, old friends and loyal dogs, plenty to eat and drink, and a perfect fire to close out the night.

A NOTE ON THE TABLE SETTING

For the cloth, I called on my old friend fabric designer Peter Fasano yet again. I knew his Kali linen, a damask-like print that I have long coveted, would be perfect for our table. I chose the fabric not just for its rich chocolate color that mirrored our main dish and dessert, but because I knew Christopher Spitzmiller's gorgeous hand-marbled plates would look stunning against it. Lucky for me, the plates debuted just before our dinner, and I've become an ardent collector. The antler candelabra, from the inimitable John Rosselli, are the perfect complement to both.

While it was a privilege to include pieces from three friends and talents I admire so enormously, I loved mixing those pieces with more humble finds: the deer antlers shed by the population that abounds in our habitat and the bird's nests I've collected for years. Heavy French bistro glasses held a Gigondas that paired beautifully with the duck, and the cane-bottomed chairs at the "Baby Doll House" made picture-perfect seats.

✧ The Menu ✧

RUM RAMSEY

HANK'S DUCK POPPERS

HOOVER DUCK

DUCK CONFIT ÉTOUFFÉE

ROASTED
BUTTERNUT SQUASH

HEARTS OF ROMAINE
with Orange, Red Onion, and
Crispy Duck Skin

BETH BIUNDO'S CHOCOLATE
RUM PECAN CAKE

DUCK DELICACIES

During duck season in the Delta, almost every man I know is up long before the sun, chasing after the mighty waterfowl before heading off to work. My friend Hank Burdine, invariably accompanied by his trusty Boykin spaniel, Boudreaux, doesn't miss a day, and his enthusiasm (and marksmanship) results in a couple of freezers full of duck meat to utilize all year long. Hank rarely turns up at a party without platters of his famous duck poppers and Hoover duck ready to go on the grill. The latter is so named because the strips of duck breast are marinated in Hoover Sauce, the creation of Hoover Lee, former mayor of Louise, Mississippi, and proprietor (with his sons Tim and Stanley) of the Lee Hong Company grocery store there. Louise is a tiny farming community, and Lee is one of the many Chinese immigrants whose families settled in the Delta in the first half of the twentieth century. His sauce is a mix of Asian and Deep South flavors and a secret so closely held, he won't mix it in front of his sons or his own wife, Freda (though Freda points out that she still gets to do the dishes). Folks who've made a close study of Hoover Sauce say it's some combo of soy sauce, onion powder, fresh garlic, cilantro, honey, and orange or lemon juice, but you can order it by phone from the store (see Sources, page 219). When Mr. Lee is out of stock, Hank falls back on Dale's Steak Seasoning, which is a lot easier to find. Also, if you are not lucky enough to have a prodigious hunter in your life, you can order the moulard duck breasts from D'Artagnan (see Sources, page 219)—the dark red meat and rich flavor come closest to the ducks we use here.

Here, I'm going to let Hank talk you through both recipes in his own words, and I'll give you the ingredients alongside.

HANK'S DUCK POPPERS

Makes 20 hors d'oeuvres

Two 4- to 6-pound whole skinless, boneless mallard duck breasts

¾ cup Hoover Sauce (see Sources, page 219) or some comparable substitute

10 large jalapeño peppers

5 applewood-smoked bacon slices

"I use wild duck only: mallard, wood duck, gadwall, teal, or widgeon. I skin and fillet the breast, and on a good-size mallard or gadwall breast, I will slice it longways three times. Wood duck and teal I only slice twice because they are smaller. Marinate the sliced duck breast for about 5 hours in Hoover Sauce. If you can't get Hoover, try a good sweet-and-sour marinade or use Dale's with some honey added to it. Or just experiment to get the taste you like.

"Slice good, big, firm jalapeños lengthwise in half after cutting the stems and ends off, and with a spoon scrape out the seeds and membranes. The membrane is where the heat is. (It doesn't hurt to leave a little membrane in a few to get a 'Sonofabitch!' exclamation around the fire pit.) Have your jalapeños sliced and ready at the prep table, along with good applewood-smoked bacon.

"Place a slice of duck in one of the pepper halves and wrap with ½ slice of bacon. Secure with a stout wooden unpainted toothpick. Grill over medium-hot coals on both sides until the bacon is a little crispy. Do not overcook. Duck should not be purple, but red in the middle. Serve off a platter to guests."

HOOVER DUCK

*Makes 20 to 30
hors d'oeuvres*

Two 4- to 6-pound whole
skinless, boneless
mallard duck breasts

¾ cup Hoover Sauce (see
Sources, page 219) or
some comparable
substitute

"Take whole duck breasts and marinate them in Hoover Sauce,
or other sweet-and-sour sauce as mentioned before, for no
longer than about 5 hours as the duck will begin to cook.

"Place on a grill over medium-hot coals. Cook with the
lid closed, 3 to 4 minutes on each side, or until the outside is
browned with grate marks burned into the breast. It is imper-
ative not to overcook. The inside of the breast should not be
purple, but a good red with bloody juices running out onto the
wooden cutting board when slicing.

"Slice the duck breasts crossways about ¼ to ½ inch thick.
Presentation looks nice when the breasts are placed sliced but
intact on the tray. Serve with
toothpicks right off of the
cutting board."

NOTE: *"It is a must if using wild
field-killed fowl to warn people that
they may encounter a steel BB or
shot in the duck. It'll break a tooth
or pop a cap right off. Be careful—I
know! Also, if someone says that
wild duck tastes too gamy, they
just don't know how to cook it. It
is a delicacy when not overcooked.
Tabasco founder E. A. McIlhenny is
reported to have said, 'The only true
way to cook a wild duck is to have
it drawn and plucked and placed
on a silver platter in the hands of a
slow-gaited butler who then walks
through a warm kitchen.' In other
words, if you overcook your duck,
feed it to your dog and go cook
some more."*

Rum Ramsey

Serves 6 to 8

Though rum is often thought of in a tropical context, it's also the perfect thing for warding off the chill of duck season—especially when combined with bourbon, which is the case in a Rum Ramsey. Invented in the 1930s, the Ramsey is little known beyond the Bon Ton Café in New Orleans, where the recipe is a closely guarded secret. The cafe's proprietor, Wayne Pierce, gave a batch to my husband one Christmas, and I've been hooked ever since. I make my Rum Ramseys with Charboneau rum (see Sources, page 219), courtesy of my pal Regina Charboneau, chef de cuisine of the American Queen Steamboat Company and seventh-generation Natchezian, as well as a cookbook author and restaurateur extraordinaire. In 2014, she and her husband, Doug, and son, Jean-Luc, started a rum distillery in Natchez's oldest building, the circa 1789 Kings Tavern. The restaurant downstairs serves up delicious fresh fish and flatbreads from the wood-fired oven, while upstairs, an enormous (and gorgeous) copper still produces rum from sugarcane grown in nearby Louisiana. Because Louisiana is also the birthplace of the Rum Ramsey, we've happily come full circle.

1½ cups white rum

1 cup bourbon

¼ cup fresh lime juice

¾ cup Simple Syrup (page 78)

½ teaspoon bitters, such as Peychaud's or The Bitter Truth Creole Bitters

Combine the rum, bourbon, lime juice, simple syrup, and bitters in a tall mixing glass or pitcher. Stir well. Pour into highball glasses filled with ice and serve.

NOTE: *For a single cocktail, combine 1½ ounces white rum, 1 ounce bourbon, ¼ ounce fresh lime juice, 2½ teaspoons simple syrup, and a dash of bitters in a mixing glass. Stir and pour into an old-fashioned glass filled with ice.*

Duck Confit Étouffée

1 teaspoon cayenne pepper

1 teaspoon salt

1 teaspoon dried thyme

¾ teaspoon freshly ground white pepper

½ teaspoon freshly ground black pepper

½ teaspoon ground all-spice

6 duck legs confit (available from D'Artagnan, see Sources, page 219)

1 cup plus 1 tablespoon Wesson oil or duck fat

3 cups andouille sausage, diced

2 cups finely chopped yellow onions

1½ cups finely chopped celery

1½ cups finely chopped green bell peppers

3 bay leaves

1 cup all-purpose flour

4 to 6 cups chicken stock

2 garlic cloves, minced

2 teaspoons Lea & Perrins Worcestershire sauce

Salt

2 tablespoons Cognac, Armagnac, or brandy

⅓ cup finely chopped scallions

'd been making duck étouffée from both wild and domestic ducks for years, and then one day, pressed for time, I grabbed a handful of duck legs confit from the meat case at my buddy Donald Link's Cochon Butcher and made the dish with them instead. Already perfectly tender and tinged with aromatics (allspice, nutmeg, juniper), they lend a depth to this dish that belies the relatively short cooking time. I've also taken a tip from the great Ken Smith (former chef at New Orleans's Upperline and now a Catholic priest), who added bits of andouille sausage to the restaurant's tasty étouffée. The spicy Cajun sausage adds further depth as well as a little heat, and I've found that the addition of Cognac or Armagnac smoothes out the flavors beautifully. At this dinner, we had some wild duck breasts left over, and I threw strips in at the last minute to good effect. No matter what you do, make a lot. (I rarely see people stop at one helping.) And serve it over cooked white rice with warm French bread on the side.

To make the seasoning mix, place the cayenne, salt, thyme, white pepper, black pepper, and allspice in a small bowl and stir to combine. Set aside.

Remove the skin from the duck legs, leaving as much fat attached to the skin as possible. Reserve the skin and refrigerate for use in the salad on page 210. Pull the duck meat off the bones and cut or tear it into large but still bite-size pieces and set aside.

In a large skillet, heat 1 tablespoon of the oil or fat over medium-high heat. Add the andouille and sauté, stirring frequently, for 5 to 8 minutes, until brown. Set aside.

Combine 1 cup of the onions, 1 cup of the celery, 1 cup of the bell peppers, and the bay leaves in a medium bowl and set aside.

In a large heavy-bottomed Dutch oven, casserole, or deep sauté pan, heat the remaining 1 cup oil or duck fat over medium-high heat until smoking hot, about 5 minutes. Gradually sprinkle in the flour, whisking with a long-handled metal whisk until smooth. Cook, whisking continuously, until the roux is a medium to dark reddish brown, 5 to 10 minutes more. Immediately add the vegetable mixture and stir well with a wooden spoon. Stir in 2 teaspoons of the seasoning mix.

Remove the pan from the heat and, 1 cup at a time, add about 4 cups of the chicken stock, stirring well to combine after each addition.

Return the pan to medium-high heat and stir in the remaining 1 cup onions, ½ cup celery, ½ cup bell peppers, and the garlic. Add the Worcestershire sauce and diced andouille and bring to a boil over high heat. Reduce the heat until the mixture stays, uncovered, at a steady simmer. Add more stock if the mixture gets too thick. (You want it to be thicker than a gumbo but not sludgy.)

Simmer for 30 minutes, stirring occasionally, and taste to see if salt or more seasoning mix is necessary. Add the duck pieces and Cognac and simmer for another 10 minutes, until the duck is heated through. Check again for seasonings, add the scallions, and simmer for about a minute more.

NOTE: *Because the étouffée only gets better with age, you can make it 2 or 3 days ahead of time and keep it, covered, in the refrigerator. It also freezes well for up to 6 months.*

Roasted Butternut Squash

There's something about the étouffée that seems to demand the sweet taste of winter squash. This roasted butternut squash is as simple as can be and adds marvelous color to the menu.

Preheat the oven to 400°F.

Place the squash cubes in a large bowl and toss with the olive oil, thyme, and sage. Season generously with salt and pepper and toss again.

Divide the squash cubes between two rectangular baking dishes. Roast for 30 to 40 minutes, tossing twice during the cooking, until tender and a little browned around the edges.

NOTE: *The squash can be roasted 4 or 5 hours beforehand and left at room temperature. Rewarm in a 400°F oven until hot, about 10 minutes.*

Serves 8 to 10

Two 3-pound butternut squash, peeled, seeded, and cut into 1-inch cubes

6 tablespoons olive oil

1 tablespoon thyme leaves

2 teaspoons chopped sage leaves

Kosher salt and freshly ground black pepper

Hearts of Romaine with Orange,
Red Onion, and Crispy Duck Skin

Reserved duck confit skin (from page 206)

3 oranges or satsumas, peeled

One 22-ounce package hearts of romaine

1 small red onion, thinly sliced

Citrus Vinaigrette

Salt and freshly ground black pepper

Makes about ¾ cup

1½ teaspoons salt

1 teaspoon sugar

2 tablespoons reserved orange juice (from above)

1 tablespoon fresh lemon juice

1 tablespoon good sherry vinegar

½ cup olive oil

Freshly ground black pepper

I n the Delta, a salad with red onions and citrus segments is a mainstay on winter tables. I made this one with oranges and the crisped skins of the étouffée's duck confit as a wink to duck à l'orange. Because this dinner took place out in the boonies, I used easy-to-find hearts of romaine, but I also happen to really like romaine's crispness with the rest of the menu. A handful of finely chopped mint leaves would be a nice addition.

Cut the reserved duck skin into strips roughly ¾ inch wide and 1½ inches long.

Add just enough water to a large skillet to come up ¼ inch along the side of the pan. Bring to a simmer over medium-high heat and add the duck skin strips. Cook, stirring occasionally, until the water evaporates, a minute or two. Turn the heat down to low and cook until the skins are crisp, being careful not to let them burn.

With a small sharp knife, slice off the tops and bases of the oranges. Stand them up and cut down their sides, following their natural curves, to remove the skins and white pith. Over a small bowl, remove the segments from the oranges by slicing between the membranes. Discard the membranes and strain the juice. Set aside both the orange segments and the juice. (The juice will be used in the vinaigrette that follows.)

Remove any ugly outer leaves from the romaine hearts and discard. Slice the hearts into 1½- to 2-inch pieces and separate the leaves. Place the leaves in a large wooden salad bowl. Add the sliced onion and orange segments and toss with the vinaigrette. Check to see if more salt and/or pepper are needed and lightly toss in the duck skins.

Citrus Vinaigrette

In a small bowl, whisk together the salt, sugar, orange juice (if the reserved juice does not add up to 2 tablespoons, squeeze some more), lemon juice, and vinegar. Whisk in the olive oil. Add pepper to taste and more salt, if needed.

Beth Biundo's Chocolate Rum Pecan Cake

Serves 8 to 10

When Beth Biundo was the pastry chef at Lilette, one of my very favorite New Orleans restaurants, more than once she made it to the finals of the James Beard Award competition for Outstanding Pastry Chef in America. When she left the restaurant to pursue a career in interior design, hearts all over town were broken, but now, thank God, she's back at the oven in her own space (see Sources, page 219). I got Beth to come up with this cake as a riff on the rum cake the mother of my best friend Jessica Brent made when we were kids. I'm pretty sure it was a Duncan Hines yellow cake with pecans baked into the top and glazed with so much rum we were always drunk. Beth's chocolate version is far more refined, but no less boozy, especially if you add all 4 tablespoons of rum to the glaze.

Preheat the oven to 350°F. Butter an 8-inch Bundt pan (or other tube pan) with a 6-cup capacity and dust all over with flour. Turn the pan upside down and tap to shake out any excess flour.

Sift together the flour, baking soda, and salt into a medium bowl. Set aside.

In the bowl of a stand mixer fitted with the whisk attachment, beat the butter until soft. Add the sugar and continue to beat for about 2 minutes. Add the eggs, one at a time, scraping the sides of the bowl as necessary and beating until thoroughly incorporated after each addition. Add the vanilla and melted chocolate and beat, scraping the sides of the bowl.

Bring the water to a boil in a small saucepan over high heat. Remove from the heat and whisk in the cocoa, continuing to whisk until it's well incorporated and the mixture is smooth. Beat the cocoa mixture into the butter-and-egg mixture. Gradually beat in about half the dry ingredients. Beat in the rum. Beat in the remaining dry ingredients.

Turn the batter into the prepared pan and smooth the top. Bake for 50 to 55 minutes, until a cake tester gently inserted comes out clean.

Let the cake cool in the pan for about 20 minutes. Cover it with a plate, and holding the plate and pan firmly together, turn them both over and remove the pan. When the cake is completely cool, pour the warm glaze over the top of the cake, allowing it to run into the grooves. Sprinkle the toasted pecans on top.

½ pound (2 sticks) butter, plus more for the pan

2 cups all-purpose flour, plus more for the pan

1 teaspoon baking soda

Pinch of kosher salt

2 cups sugar

3 large eggs

1 teaspoon pure vanilla extract

6 ounces bittersweet chocolate, melted and cooled

2 tablespoons cocoa powder

½ cup water

¾ cup dark rum

Chocolate Rum Glaze (recipe follows)

Toasted Pecans (recipe follows)

NOTE: This cake is plenty good on its own, but it wouldn't hurt to serve it with vanilla or butter pecan ice cream on the side, or whipped cream enlivened with a bit of rum. We especially enjoyed ours with shot glasses of aged dark rum (15-year-old Barbancourt Estate Reserve is a special favorite).

Chocolate Rum Glaze

Place the chocolate in a small heatproof bowl.

In a small saucepan, bring the cream and butter to a simmer over medium-high heat, whisking to melt and blend the butter.

Remove the mixture from the heat and immediately pour it over the chocolate. Stir continuously until the chocolate has melted. Stir in as much rum as desired. While the glaze is still warm, pour it over the cooled cake.

Toasted Pecans

Preheat the oven to 350°F.

Place the pecans in a shallow baking pan in the middle of the oven for 12 to 15 minutes, stirring occasionally. They should be very hot, but should not darker in color.

When cool enough to handle, chop the pecans roughly and sprinkle them over the glazed cake while the glaze is still warm.

Makes about 1 ½ cups

- **3** ounces bittersweet chocolate, roughly chopped
- ½ cup heavy cream
- **2** tablespoons butter
- **2** to **4** tablespoons dark rum

Makes about ¾ cup

- ¾ cup pecan halves

ACKNOWLEDGMENTS

So many people—friends, family, fellow cooks, festive guests—made this book a joy to work on and I am grateful to them all. Special thanks go to the following: Paul Costello, who created the gorgeous images on these pages, was the most intrepid and always game road-trip companion a girl could have. Now that we're done, I cannot imagine having embarked on this project with anyone else. His brilliant wife, Sara, provided inspiration, encouragement, and an infallible eye. Alex Darsey, Paul's sometime assistant and a talented photographer in his own right, joined us for part of the ride, during which he worked tirelessly and always added to the fun.

I had the privilege of working with the ever tasteful Sandy Gilbert Freidus on *One Man's Folly: The Exceptional Houses of Furlow Gatewood,* and from that happy experience this project was born. Sandy is a whip-smart editor, supremely patient cheerleader, and, now, valued friend.

Fearn and Roberto de Vicq de Cumptich, our gifted designers, totally "got" the project, the region, and the feeling I wanted to impart about it from the start. Their work is as inventive, intuitive, and lovely as they are and I owe them a huge debt.

My dear friends Peter Patout, Jon and Keith Meacham, and Libby and Ben Page opened their houses to me for this book, as they do in real life. Eustace Winn's stewardship of the Hollywood Plantation has ensured that the Delta has another magical setting in which to entertain.

Peter Fasano and Elizabeth Hamilton printed fabulous fabrics on a moment's notice and are the most splendidly supportive pals.

Hank Burdine served as fire builder, chief sandbar wrangler, whiskey provider, dove hunt organizer, and wild duck chef extraordinaire. He greeted every crazy idea I had with more enthusiasm and generosity than I can ever repay.

Howard Brent, Sid ("Bo Weevil") Law, and Raymond Longoria were stalwart riverboat captains and sandbar hosts. Hank, Howard, Raymond, and the beloved Brent Sisters (Jessica, Eden, and Bronwynne) also provided a boatload of music and joy.

Mary Sferruzza and Robert Jenkins have been much loved culinary and design mentors for as long as I can remember. Sherry and Sarah Smythe helped me out of many a tight spot and enhance any event they throw or attend.

Frank Liger manages my family's collective life with finesse, love, and astounding energy. Not much would happen without him, including most of the parties on these pages—or the stunning Christmas tree he creates for me every year. Florence Boston enhances all our existences with her care, competence, and grace.

Rosemary Russ—along with her mother Rosana Johnson, her sister Frankie Johnson, and her nephew Terrell Johnson—has helped me throw more parties than I can count. There's no one I'd rather hang out in a kitchen with more than Rose.

Julie Trice and Lisa Rogers, with boundless patience and good humor, kept me organized on and off the road.

I also want to thank Charles Miers, publisher of Rizzoli, for embracing this book; my husband, John Pearce, for putting up with the chaos; and Mama and Daddy, always, for showing me how it's done.

All of the above make "my South" the place I love the most.

SOURCES

Most of the resources here have been mentioned in the text. All of them stock things I use constantly, from the antique wine rinsers and finger bowls in which I love to arrange flowers (Hollyhock and KRB) to colorful inexpensive glassware and Limoges goblets (Found).

TABLETOP

Barn Light Electric Co.
(800) 407-8784
barnlightelectric.com
Beautiful porcelain enamelware plates, cups, and bowls.

Christopher Spitzmiller, Inc.
979 Third Avenue, Suite 1818
New York, New York 10022
(212) 563-3030
christopherspitzmiller.com

Corzine & Co.
4003 Hillsboro Pike
Nashville, Tennessee 37215
(615) 385-0140
corzineco.com
Founded by my late uncle, Michael Corzine, this shop remains my go-to source for china (including Herend), crystal from Baccarat and William Yeoward, glassware (like the Simon Pearce Revere bowl on pages 158 and 175), linens, and much, much more.

Creel and Gow
131 East 70th Street
New York, New York 10021
(212) 327-4281
creelandgow.com

Found
3433 West Alabama Street
Houston, Texas 77027
(713) 522-9191
shop.foundforthehome.com

Hollyhock
927 North La Cienega Boulevard
Los Angeles, California 90069
(310) 777-0100
hollyhockinc.com

John Rosselli Antiques
306 East 61st Street
New York, New York 10065
(212) 750-0060
johnrosselliantiques.com

KRB
135½ East 79th Street
New York, New York 10075
(212) 288-2221
krbnyc.com

Lagniappe Fine Gifts
1361 East Reed Road
Greenville, Mississippi 38703
(662) 335-3722
and
1300 Van Buren, Suite 109
Oxford, Mississippi 38655
(662) 638-3419
lagniappefinegifts.com

Sherry and Sarah Smythe's inviting spaces feature everything from art (including works by Joan Griswold and William Dunlap) to Matouk linens and Herend china.

Lucullus
610 Chartres Street
New Orleans, Louisiana 70130
(504) 528-9620
lucullusantiques.com
Patrick Dunne has assembled an extensive collection of culinary antiques, from copper cookware and silver serving pieces to nineteenth-century stemware, oversize monogrammed napkins, and porcelain, including the cornflower garland pattern used for "A Jeffersonian Evening," page 160.

McCartys Pottery
101 Saint Mary's Street
Merigold, Mississippi 38759
(662) 748-2293
mccartyspottery.com

Robert DuGrenier Associates, Inc.
1096 Vermont Route 30
Townshend, Vermont 05353
(802) 365-4400
dugrenier.com
A glassblower specializing in custom orders, including the highballs on page 94 as well as the tortoiseshell versions on page 204.

William-Wayne & Co.
846 Lexington Avenue
New York, New York 10065
(800) 318-3435
william-wayne.com

FABRIC

Architextiles
architextiles.com

Peter Fasano, Ltd.
peterfasano.com

PAPER

Erika Jack
erikajack.com

Scriptura
5423 Magazine Street
New Orleans, Louisiana 70115
(504) 897-1555
scriptura.com
Margaret and Sallie Jones are miracle workers who create gorgeous invitations and menu cards from any image I give them, whether it's the Jack Spencer photo on page 52 or the Joan Griswold painting on page 180. The best source for all things paper.

FOOD, WINE, AND SPIRITS

Benton's Smoky Mountain Country Hams
2603 Highway 411 North
Madisonville, Tennessee 37354
(423) 442-5003
bentonscountryhams2.com

Beth Biundo Sweets
(504) 782-9736
bethbiundosweets.com

Charboneau Distillery
617 Jefferson Street
Natchez, Mississippi 39120
(601) 861-4203
charboneaudistillery.com

D'Artagnan
(800) 327-8246
dartagnan.com

Fee Brothers
feebrothers.com

Keife & Co.
801 Howard Avenue
New Orleans, Louisiana 70113
(504) 523-7272
keifeandco.com
Owners Jim Yonkus and John Keife were my advisors on the wines for the bulk of the parties here, as they are pretty much every day! They also carry a phenomenal range of spirits and a well-sourced array of bitters, cured meats, cheeses, olives, chocolates, salts—in short everything you need for a well-stocked bar and pantry.

Lee Hong Company
1294 Main Street
Louise, Mississippi 39097
(662) 836-5131

Sister Schubert's
sisterschuberts.com

Taste of Gourmet
(800) 833-7731
tasteofgourmet.com

ENTERTAINMENT

Eden Brent
Little Boogaloo Entertainment, LLC
(662) 347-2667
edenbrent.com

INDEX

Page numbers in *italic* indicate illustrations.

A

Aioli, Fennel, *80*, 81
Almond
  Buttermilk Shortcakes with Peaches Poached in Red Wine and White Chocolate Whipped Cream, *108*, 109–110
  Polenta Cake with Coconut Ice Cream and Candied Citrus, *30*, 31
Asparagus with Brown Butter Vinaigrette, 28, *29*

B

Bacon
  Brown Sugar, *136*, 137
  in Field Pea and Rice Salad, 64–65, *65*
  Watermelon Pickles, -Wrapped, 56, *57*
Beef
  Daube Glacé, 44, *45*
  Rib-eye Roast, *148*, 149
  Tenderloin with Hot Mustard and Horseradish Sauce, *190*, 191–192
Biscuits, 54, 71
Bitters, 78
  Grapefruit, Champagne Cocktails with, *16*, 17
Blackberry Cobbler, Mary Mack's, *66*, 67
Bourbon
  Balls, *194*, 195
  in Rum Ramsey, *204*, 205
  in Whiskey Sours, Frozen, *182*, 183
Bread Pudding
  Cheese Soufflé, Mock, *26*, 27
  Mushroom, 134, *135*
Brent, Eden, 68–69, 183, 219
Brown Butter Vinaigrette,

Asparagus with, 28, *29*
Brown Sugar Bacon, *136*, 137
Bruschetta with Fig Relish and Burata, *96*, 97
Burata, Bruschetta with Fig Relish and, 96, 97
Butternut Squash, Roasted, 209

C

Café au Lait Pots de Crème, 50, *51*
Cake(s)
  Almond Polenta, with Coconut Ice Cream and Candied Citrus, *30*, 31
  Chocolate Rum Pecan, Beth Biundo's, *212*, 213–214
Canapés
  Cheese Dreams, *184*, 185
  Corn Cakes with Crème Fraîche and Trout Roe, *18*, 19
  Corn Muffins, Mini, with Smoked Salmon and Dill Crème Fraîche, *184*, 186
  Ham Gougères, Deviled, *184*, 187
Candied Citrus, *30*, 31
Celery Root Rémoulade, 48
Celery Seed Dressing, 138
Champagne
  Cocktails with Grapefruit Bitters, *16*, 17
  The Evening Storm, 116–117, *117*
  fried chicken pairing, 72
  Pimm's Royale, *38*, 39
Cheese
  Bruschetta with Fig Relish and Burata, *96*, 97
  and Crab Sandwiches, Grilled Deviled, 40, *41*
  Dreams, *184*, 185
  Gougères, Deviled Ham, *184*, 187
  Macaroni, Gratin de, 170, *171*
  Soufflé, Mock, *26*, 27
Chess Pie Squares, *124*, 125

Chicken
  Breast, Sliced, with Tomato Vinaigrette, 106–107, *107*
  Fried, *60*, 61
  fried, takeout, 71–72
Chocolate
  Bourbon Balls, *194*, 195
  Rum Glaze, 214
  Rum Pecan Cake, Beth Biundo's, *212*, 213–214
  Sauce, 174
  White, Whipped Cream, 110
Christmas cocktail supper. *See* Cocktail Supper, Christmas
Citrus
  Candied, *30*, 31
  Vinaigrette, 210
Cobbler, Blackberry, Mary Mack's, *66*, 67
Cocktails. *See also* Simple Syrup
  Champagne, with Grapefruit Bitters, *16*, 17
  The Evening Storm, 116–117, *117*
  Lemonade with Vodka, Lavender Mint, 56, 57
  Pimm's Royale, *38*, 39
  Pink Perfection, *94*, 95
  resources for, 219
  Rum Ramsey, *204*, 205
  The Saint Cloud, *131*, 131
  The Southside, 77, 78
  Whiskey Sours, Frozen, *182*, 183
Cocktail supper, Christmas, 176–181
  decorations, *180*, 181, *181*
  menu, 177–178
  table setting, *176*, 177
Consommé Rice Pilaf, 155, 157
Corn, Deconstructed Street Corn, *122*, 123
Corn Cakes with Crème Fraîche and Trout Roe, *18*, 19
Corn Muffins, Mini, with Smoked Salmon and

Dill Crème Fraîche, *184*, 186
Crab(meat)
    and Cheese Sandwiches, Grilled
        Deviled, 40, *41*
    Jumbo Lump, Green Goddess Soup
        with, *82*, 83
    Mornay with Toast Points, *189*, 189
    Norfolk, 166, *167*
    Soup, Creole, 20, *21*
Crackers, Saltines, Baked, *119*, 120
Crème Fraîche
    Corn Cakes with Trout Roe and, *18*,
        19
    Dill, Mini Corn Muffins with
        Smoked Salmon and, *184*, 186
    in Macaroni, Gratin de, 170, *171*
Creole
    Crab Soup, 20, *21*
    defined, 33
    Rémoulade Sauce, 46, *47*
Creole cold supper, 32–37
Curry Dip, *184*, 188

D

Daube Glacé, 44, *45*
Desserts
    Almond Buttermilk Shortcakes
        with Peaches Poached in
        Red Wine and White Chocolate
        Whipped Cream, *108*, 109–110
    Almond Polenta Cake with
        Coconut Ice Cream and Candied
        Citrus, *30*, 31
    Blackberry Cobbler, Mary Mack's,
        66, 67
    Bourbon Balls, *194*, 195
    Charlotte Russe, *158*, 159
    Chess Pie Squares, *124*, 125
    Chocolate Rum Pecan Cake, Beth
        Biundo's, *212*, 213–214
    Ice Cream, Pineapple Mint,
        Justine's, 86, *87*
    Pots de Crème, Café au Lait, 50, *51*
    Profiteroles with Chocolate Sauce,
        174, 175
Dip(s)
    Aioli, Fennel, *80*, 81

Curry, *184*, 188
    Mayonnaise, Sriracha, 58, *59*
Duck
    Confit Étouffée, 206–208, *207*
    Hoover, 200, *202*, 202
    Poppers, Hank's, 200, *201*, 201
    Skin, Crispy, Hearts of Romaine
        with Orange, Red Onion, and,
        210, *211*
Duck dinner, Hollywood Plantation,
    196–199
    menu, 199
    table setting, *198*, 199

E

Étouffée, Duck Confit, 206–208, *207*
Evening Storm, The, 116–117, *117*

F

Fall hunt breakfast, 128–130
    menu, 130
    table setting, *128*, 129
Fasano, Peter, 90, 129, 198, 219
Fennel Aioli, *80*, 81
Fig Relish, Bruschetta with Buratta
    and, 96, *97*
Fish
    Salmon, Smoked, Mini Corn
        Muffins with Dill Crème Fraîche
        and, *184*, 186
    Trout Roe, Corn Cakes with Crème
        Fraîche and, *18*, 19
    Trout, Smoked, and Sweet Potato
        Hash, *132*, 133
Food sources, 219
Fritters, Okra, with Sriracha
    Mayonnaise, 58, *59*
Fruit, Fresh, with Celery Seed
    Dressing, 138, *139*

G

Gazpacho with Tomato Sherbet, *98*,
    99–100
Gin, in The Southside, 78
Glaze, Chocolate Rum, 214
Gougères, Deviled Ham, *184*, 187
Grapefruit

Bitters, Champagne Cocktails with,
    16, 17
The Saint Cloud, *131*, 131
Green Beans, Haricots Verts with
    Shallot Vinaigrette, *49*, 49
Green Goddess Soup with Jumbo
    Lump Crabmeat, *82*, 83
Gus's World Famous Fried Chicken, 72

H

Ham
    with biscuits, 54, *70*
    in Crab Norfolk, 166, *167*
    Field Pea and Rice Salad, 64–65, *65*
    Gougères, Deviled, *184*, 187
Hank's Duck Poppers, 200, *201*, 201
Haricots Verts, with Shallot
    Vinaigrette, *49*, 49
Harling, Robert, 75, 90, 144
Hash, Smoked Trout and Sweet
    Potato, *132*, 133
Hollywood Plantation duck dinner.
    See Duck dinner, Hollywood
    plantation
Hoover Duck, 200, *202*, 202
Hoover Sauce, 200, 201, 219
Hors d'oeuvres. *See also* Canapés;
    Sandwiches
    Asparagus with Curry Dip, *184*, 188
    Bruschetta with Fig Relish and
        Burata, 96, *97*
    Crabmeat Mornay with Toast
        Points, *189*, 189
    Duck, Hoover, 200, *202*, 202
    Duck Poppers, Hank's, 200, *201*, 201
    Okra Fritters with Sriracha
        Mayonnaise, 58, *59*
    Oysters, Fried, with Fennel Aioli,
        80, 81
    Oysters, Fried, in Romaine Canoes,
        42, *43*
    Oysters Rockefeller, 79, *80*
    Shrimp, Marinated, 118, *119*
    Watermelon Pickles, Bacon-
        Wrapped, 56, *57*
Horseradish
    Mousse, *152*, 153

Sauce, 192

I

Ice Cream
    Coconut, Almond Polenta Cake
        with Candied Citrus and, *30, 31*
    Pineapple Mint, Justine's, 86, *87*
    in Profiteroles with Chocolate
        Sauce, 174, *175*

J

Jack, Erika, 147, 219
Jeffersonian evening, 160–165
    historical basis for, 161–162, *163*
    menu, 163
    table setting, *160*, 164

L

Lamb
    Bourguignon, 168–170, *169*
    Leg of, Roasted Boneless, with
        Herbs, 24, *25*
    Stock, Homemade, 22
Lavender Mint Lemonade with
    Vodka, 56, *57*
Lemonade with Vodka, Lavender
    Mint, 56, *57*

M

Macaroni, Gratin de, 170, *171*
Madeira, 37
Maltaise Sauce, Blender, *132*, 133
Mary B's Biscuits, 71
Mayonnaise, Sriracha, 58, *59*
McHardy's Chicken and Fixin',
    New Orleans, 72
Meacham, Keith and Jon, 53–54, 67,
    71, 161, 165
Mint
    Lavender Lemonade with Vodka,
        56, *57*
    Pineapple Ice Cream, Justine's, 86,
        87
    Potatoes, New, with Garlic and, *122,
        123*
Mississippi sandbar picnic, 112–115
    menu, 113–114, *115*

playlist, 114
Mousse
    Horseradish, *152*, 153
    Mustard, Mary's, *150*, 151
Muffins, Mini Corn, with Smoked
    Salmon and Dill Crème Fraîche,
    184, 186
Mushroom Bread Pudding, 134, *135*
Mustard
    Hot, *190*, 191
    Mousse, Mary's, *150*, 151
    Sherry Vinaigrette, *172*, 173

O

Okra Fritters with Sriracha
    Mayonnaise, 58, *59*
Orange(s)
    Candied Citrus, *30, 31*
    Hearts of Romaine with Red Onion,
        Crispy Duck Skin, and, 210, *211*
    Maltaise Sauce, Blender, *132*, 133
    Rum, -Infused, 95
    Vinaigrette, Citrus, 210
    Whiskey Sours, Frozen, *182*, 183
Oysters
    Fried, with Fennel Aioli, *80*, 81
    Fried, in Romaine Canoes, *42, 43*
    Rockefeller, 79, *80*
    Scalloped, 154, *155*

P

Page, Ben and Libby, 89
Paper sources, 147, 219
Peaches Poached in Red Wine,
    Almond Buttermilk Shortcakes
    with White Chocolate Whipped
    Cream and, *108*, 109–110
Peas
    Butter Lettuce, and Herbs, Salad of,
        172, 173
    Field Pea and Rice Salad, 64–65, *65*
Pecan(s)
    in Bourbon Balls, *194*, 195
    Chocolate Rum Cake, Beth
        Biundo's, *212*, 213–214
    Toasted, 214
Pickles, Watermelon, Bacon-

    Wrapped, 56, *57*
Pilaf, Consommé Rice, *155*, 157
Pimm's Royale, *38*, *39*
Pineapple
    The Evening Storm, 116–117
    Mint Ice Cream, Justine's, 86, *87*
Pink Perfection, *94*, 95
Playlist, 68–69, 114
Polenta Cake, Almond, with Coconut
    Ice Cream and Candied Citrus,
    30, 31
Pork. *See also* Bacon; Ham
    Shoulder, Barbecued, *120*, 121
Potatoes
    in Hash, Smoked Trout and Sweet
        Potato, *132, 133*
    New, with Garlic and Mint, *122, 123*
Prince's Hot Chicken, Nashville, 71–72
Profiteroles with Chocolate Sauce,
    174, *175*
Pudding Soufflés, Zucchini, with
    Creamy Tomato Sauce, 101–102,
    102, 103

R

Relish, Fig, Bruschetta with Buratta
    and, 96, *97*
Rémoulade Sauce
    Creole, 46, *47*
    White, 48
Rib-eye Roast, *148*, 149
Rice
    and Field Pea Salad, 64–65, *65*
    Pilaf, Consommé, *155*, 157
    Shrimp Malacca with, 84, *85*
Romaine
    Canoes, Fried Oysters in, *42, 43*
    Hearts of, with Orange, Red Onion,
        and Crispy Duck Skin, 210, *211*
Rosemary Simple Syrup, 131
Rosé wines, 93
Rum
    Chocolate Glaze, 214
    Chocolate Pecan Cake, Beth
        Biundo's, *212*, 213–214
    The Evening Storm, 116–117
    Orange-Infused, 95

Pink Perfection, *94*, 95
Ramsey, *204*, 205

S

Saint Cloud, The, *131*, 131
Salad(s)
    of Butter Lettuce, Peas, and Herbs,
        172, *173*
    Field Pea and Rice, 64–65, *65*
    Fruit, Fresh, with Celery Seed
        Dressing, 138, *139*
    Romaine, Hearts of, with Orange,
        Red Onion, and Crispy Duck
        Skin, 210, *211*
Salmon, Smoked, Mini Corn Muffins
    with Dill Crème Fraîche and, *184*,
    186
Saltines, Baked, *119*, 120
Sandwiches
    Beef Tenderloin with Hot Mustard
        and Horseradish Sauce, *190*,
        191–192
    Crab and Cheese, Grilled Deviled,
        40, *41*
Sauce(s)
    Chocolate, 174
    Hoover, 200
    Horseradish, 192
    Maltaise, Blender, *132*, 133
    Rémoulade, Creole, *46*, 47
    Rémoulade, White, 48
    Tomato, Creamy, 102, *103*
Shallot Vinaigrette, Haricots Verts
    with, *49*, 49
Shellfish. *See* Crab(meat); Oysters;
    Shrimp
Shellfish dinner, 74–76
Sherbet, Tomato, *98*, 100
Sherry Mustard Vinaigrette, 172, *173*
Shortcakes, Almond Buttermilk, with
    Peaches Poached in Red Wine and
    White Chocolate Whipped Cream,
    108, 109–110
Shrimp
    Malacca with Rice, *84*, 85
    Marinated, 118, *119*
    Rémoulade, *46*, 47

Stock, Homemade, 22
Simple Syrup, 78
    Lavender, 56
    Rosemary, 131
Sister Schubert's, 71, 129, 191, 219
Soufflé(s)
    Cheese, Mock, *26*, 27
    Zucchini Pudding, with Creamy
        Tomato Sauce, 101–102, *102*, *103*
Soup(s). *See also* Stock
    Crab, Creole, *20*, 21
    Gazpacho with Tomato Sherbet, *98*,
        99–100
    Green Goddess, with Jumbo Lump
        Crabmeat, *82*, 83
Southside, The, *77*, 78
Spencer, Jack, 54
Spinach, Jason's, *155*, 156
Spitzmiller, Christopher, 198, 218
Spring lunch, 11–15
Squash, Butternut, Roasted, 209
Sriracha Mayonnaise, 58, *59*
Stock
    Lamb, Homemade, 22
    Shrimp, Homemade, 22
Summer lawn celebration, 52–55,
    68–73
    biscuits/fried chicken takeout,
    71–72
    champagne selection, 72
    entertainment, 68–69
    menu, 55
Summer Squash Casserole, Nancy
    Peterkin's, 62, *63*
Sweet Potato and Smoked Trout Hash,
    132, 133

T

Table setting resources, 218–219
Tarte Tatin, Tomato, *104*, 105
Toast Points, 189
Tomato(es)
    Gazpacho with Tomato Sherbet,
        98, 99–100
    Sauce, Creamy, 102, *103*
    Sherbet, *98*, 100
    Slow-Roasted, *136*, 137

Tarte Tatin, *104*, 105
    Vinaigrette, Sliced Chicken Breast
        with, 106–107, *107*
Tomatopalooza dinner, 88–93
    menu, 91
    table setting, *90*, 90
    wine selection, 93
Trout
    Roe, Corn Cakes with Crème
        Fraîche and, *18*, 19
    Smoked, and Sweet Potato Hash,
        132, 133

V

Vinaigrette
    Brown Butter, Asparagus with, 28,
        29
    Citrus, 210
    in Field Pea and Rice Salad, 64–65,
        65
    Shallot, Haricots Verts with, *49*, 49
    Sherry Mustard, 172, *173*
    Tomato, Sliced Chicken Breast
        with, 106–107, *107*
Visiting Dignitary dinner
    menu, 141–142, *143*
    table setting, *140*, *145*, *147*, *150*
Vodka
    Lavender Mint Lemonade with,
        56, *57*
The Saint Cloud, *131*, 131

W

Watermelon
    Juice, 95
    Pickles, Bacon-Wrapped, 56, *57*
Whipped Cream, White Chocolate,
    110
Whiskey Sours, Frozen, *182*, 183
White Chocolate Whipped Cream, 110
Wine resources, 14, 72, 219

Z

Zucchini Pudding Soufflés with
    Creamy Tomato Sauce, 101–102,
    102, *103*

First published in the United States of America in 2016
by Rizzoli International Publications, Inc.
300 Park Avenue South
New York, New York 10010
www.rizzoliusa.com

Text © 2016 by Julia Reed
Photography © 2016 by Paul Costello

2016 2017 2018 2019/ 10 9 8 7 6 5 4 3 2

Printed in China

ISBN 13: 978-0-8478-4828-7

Library of Congress Control Number: 2015958266

Project Editor: Sandra Gilbert
Art Direction & Design: Fearn Cutler de Vicq & Roberto de Vicq de Cumptich
Production: Maria Pia Gramaglia